William Hepworth Dixon

Free Russia

William Hepworth Dixon

Free Russia

ISBN/EAN: 9783742836236

Manufactured in Europe, USA, Canada, Australia, Japa

Cover: Foto ©Andreas Hilbeck / pixelio.de

Manufactured and distributed by brebook publishing software (www.brebook.com)

William Hepworth Dixon

Free Russia

COLLECTION
OF
BRITISH AUTHORS

TAUCHNITZ EDITION.

VOL. 1273.

FREE RUSSIA BY WILLIAM HEPWORTH DIXON.

IN TWO VOLUMES.

VOL. II.

FREE RUSSIA.

BY

WILLIAM HEPWORTH DIXON.

COPYRIGHT EDITION.

IN TWO VOLUMES.
VOL. II.

LEIPZIG
BERNHARD TAUCHNITZ
1872.

CONTENTS

OF VOLUME II.

		Page
CHAPTER I.	Roads	7
— II.	A Peasant Poet	15
— III.	Forest Scenes	23
— IV.	Patriarchal Life	32
— V.	Village Republics	42
— VI.	Communism	50
— VII.	Towns	57
— VIII.	Kief	64
— IX.	Panslavonia	69
— X.	Exile	75
— XI.	The Siberians	84
— XII.	St. George	93
— XIII.	Novgorod the Great	101
— XIV.	Serfage	107
— XV.	A Tartar Court	113
— XVI.	St. Philip	119
— XVII.	Serfs	126
— XVIII.	Emancipation	134
— XIX.	Freedom	142
— XX.	Tsek and Artel	151

CONTENTS OF VOLUME II.

			Page
CHAPTER XXI.	Masters and Men		161
— XXII.	The Bible		169
— XXIII.	Parish Priests		176
— XXIV.	A Conservative Revolution		184
— XXV.	Secret Police		194
— XXVI.	Provincial Rulers		203
— XXVII.	Open Courts		213
— XXVIII.	Islam		223
— XXIX.	The Volga		232
— XXX.	Eastern Steppe		241
— XXXI.	Don Kozaks		250
— XXXII.	Under Arms		257
— XXXIII.	Alexander		266

FREE RUSSIA.

CHAPTER I.

Roads.

A MAN who loads himself with common luggage would find these Russian roads rather rough, whether his journey lay through the forest or across the steppe. An outfit for a journey is a work of art. A hundred things, useful to the traveller, are needed on these roads, from candle and cushion down to knife and fork; but there are two things which he cannot live without—a tea-pot and a bed.

My line from the Arctic Sea to the southern slopes of the Ural range; from the straits of Yeni Kale to the Gulf of Riga; runs over land and lake, forest and fen, hill and steppe. My means of travel are those of the country; drojki, cart, barge, tarantass, steamer, sledge and train. The first stage of my journey from north to south is from Solovetsk to Archangel; made in the provision boat, under the eyes of Father John. This stage is easy, the grouping picturesque, the weather good, and the voyage accomplished in the allotted time. The second stage is from Archangel to Vietegra; done by posting in five or six days and nights; a drive of eight hundred versts, through one vast forest of birch and pine. My cares set in at this second stage. There is trouble about the podorojna; paper signed by the police, giving you a right to claim horses at the posting stations at a regulated price. As very few persons drive to Holmogory, the police make a fuss about my papers, wondering why the gentleman could not sail in a boat up the Dvina like other folk, instead of tearing through a region in which there is hardly any road. Wish to see the birthplace of Lomonosoff! What is there to see? A log-cabin, a poor town, a scrubby country —that is all! Yet after some delays the police give in, the paper is signed. Then comes the question:—carriage, cart, or sledge? No public vehicle runs to the capital; nothing but a light cart, just big enough to hold a bag of letters and a boy. That cart goes twice a-week through the forest tracks, but no one save the boy in charge can ride with the imperial mail. A stranger has to find his means of getting forward, and his choice is limited to a cart, a tarantass, and a sledge.

"A sledge is the thing," says a voice at my elbow; "but to use a sledge you must wait until the snow is deep and the frost sets in. In summer we have no roads; in some long reaches not a path; but from the day when we get five degrees of frost, we have the noblest roads in the world."

"That may be six or seven weeks hence?"

"Yes, true; then you must have a tarantass. Come over with me to the maker's yard."

A tarantass is a better sort of cart, with the addition of splash-board, hood, and step. It has no springs; for a carriage slung on steel could not be sent through these desert wastes. A spring might snap; and a broken coach, some thirty or forty miles from the nearest hamlet, is a vehicle in which very few people would like to trust their feet. A good coach is a sight to see; but a good coach implies a smooth road, with a blacksmith's forge at every turn. A man with rubles in his purse can do many things; but a man with a million rubles in his purse could not venture to drive through forest and steppe in a carriage which no one in the country could repair.

A tarantass lies lightly on a raft of poles; mere lengths of green pine, cut down and trimmed with a peasant's axe, and lashed on the axles of two pairs of wheels, some nine or ten feet apart. The body is an empty shell, into which you drop your trunks and traps, and then fill up with hay and straw. A leather blind and apron to match, keep out a little of the rain; not much; for the drifts and squalls defy all efforts to shut them out. The thing is light and airy, needing no skill to make and mend. A pole may split as you jolt along; you stop in the forest skirt, cut down a pine, smooth off the leaves and twigs; and there, you have another pole! All damage is repaired in half-an-hour.

On scanning this vehicle closely in and out,

my mind is clear that the drive to St. Petersburg should be done in a tarantass—not in a common cart. But I am dreaming all this while that the tarantass before me can be hired. A sad mistake! No maker can be found to part from his carriage on any terms short of purchase out and out. "St. Petersburg is a long way off," says he; "how shall I get my tarantass back?"

"By sending your man along with it. Charge me for his time, and let him bring it home."

The maker shakes his head.

"Too far! Will you send him to Vietegra, near the lake?"

"No," says the man, after some little pause, "not even to Vietegra. You see, when you pay off my man, he has still to get back; his journey will be worse than yours, on account of the autumn rains; he may sink in the marsh; he may stick in the sand; not to speak of his being robbed by bandits, and devoured by wolves."

"He is not afraid of robbers and wolves?"

"Why not? The forests are full of wild men, runaways, and thieves; and three weeks hence the wolves will be out in packs. How, then, can he be sure of getting home with my tarantass?"

Things look as though the vehicle must be bought. How much will it cost? A strong tarantass is said to be worth three hundred and fifty rubles. But the waste of money is not all. What can you do with it, when it is yours? A tarantass in these northern forests is like the white elephant in the

Eastern story. "Can one sell such a thing in Vietegra?"

"Ha, ha!" laughs my friend. "In Vietegra, the people are not fools; in fact, they are rather sharp ones. They will say they have no use for a tarantass; they know you can't wait to chaffer about the price. Your best plan will be to drive into a station, pay the driver, and run away."

"Leaving my tarantass in the yard?"

"Exactly; that will be cheaper in the end. Some years ago I drove to Vietegra in a fine tarantass; no one would buy it from me. One fellow offered me ten kopeks. Enraged at his impudence, I put up my carriage in a yard to be kept for me; and every six months I received a bill for rent. In ten years time that tarantass had cost me thrice its original price. In vain I begged the man to sell it; no buyer could be found. I offered to give it him, out and out; he declined my gift. At length I sent a man to fetch it home; but when my servant got to Vietegra he could find neither keeper nor tarantass. He only learned that in years gone by the yard was closed and my tarantass sold with the other traps."

A God-speed dinner is the happy means of lifting this cloud of trouble from my mind. "The man," says our helpful Consul, "thinks he will never see his tarantass again. Now, take my servant, Dimitri, with you; he is a clever fellow, not afraid of wolves and runaways; he may be trusted to bring it safely back."

"If Dimitri goes with you," adds a friendly

merchant, "I will lend you my tarantass; it is strong and roomy; big enough for two."

You will! A grip of hands, a flutter of thanks, and the thing is done.

"Why, now," cries my host, "you will travel like a Tsar."

This private tarantass is brought round to the gates; an empty shell, into which they toss our luggage; first the hard pieces—hat-box, gun-case, trunk; then piles of hay to fill up chinks and holes, and wisps of straw to bind the mass; on all of which they lay your bedding, coats and skins. A woodman's axe, a coil of rope, a ball of string, a bag of nails, a pot of grease, a basket of bread and wine, a joint of roast beef, a tea-pot, and a case of cigars are afterwards coaxed into nooks and crannies of the shell.

Starting at dusk, so as to reach the ferry, at which you are to cross the river by day-break, we plash the mud and grind the planks of Archangel beneath our hoofs. "Good-bye! Look out for wolves! Take care of brigands! Good-bye, Good-bye!" shout a dozen voices; and then that friendly and frozen city is left behind.

All night, under murky stars, we tear along a dreary path; pines on our right, pines on our left, and pines in our front. We bump through a village, waking up houseless dogs; we reach a ferry, and pass the river on a raft; we grind over stones and sand; we tug through slush and bog; all night, all day; all night again, and after that, all day; winding through the maze of forest leaves, now burnt and sear, and swirling on every blast that blows. Each day of our drive is like its fellow. A clearing, thirty yards wide, runs out before us for a thousand versts. The pines are all alike, the birches all alike. The villages are still more like each other than the trees. Our only change is in the track itself, which passes from sandy rifts to slimy beds, from grassy fields to rolling logs. In a thousand versts we count a hundred versts of log, two hundred versts of sand, three hundred versts of grass, four hundred versts of water-way and marsh.

We smile at the Russians for laying down lines of rail in districts where they have neither a turnpike road nor a country lane. But how are they to blame? An iron path is the natural way in forest lands, where stone in scarce, as is Russia and the United States.

If the sands are bad, the logs are worse. One night we spend in a kind of protest; dreaming that our luggage has been badly packed, and that on daylight coming, it shall be laid in some easier way. The trunk calls loudly for a change. My seat by day, my bed by night, this box has a leading part in our little play; but no adjustment of the other traps, no stuffing in of hay and straw, no coaxing of the furs and skins suffice to appease the fretful spirit of that trunk. It slips and jerks beneath me; rising in pain at every plunge. Coaxing it with skins is useless; soothing it with wisps of straw is vain. We tie it with bands and belts; but nothing will induce it to lie down. How can we blame it? Trunks have rights as well as men; they claim a proper place to lie in; and my poor box has just been tossed into this tarantass, and told to lie quiet on logs and stones.

Still more fretful than this trunk are the lumbâr vertebræ in my spine. They hate this jolting day and night; but these mutineers are under more control than the trunk; and when they begin to murmur seriously, I still them in a moment by hints of taking them for a drive through Bitter Creek.

Ha—here is Holmogory! Standing on a bluff above the river, pretty and bright, with her golden cross, her grassy roads, her pink and white houses, her boats on the water, and her stretches of yellow sands; a village with open spaces; here a church, there a cloister; gay with gilt and paint, and shanties of a better class than you see in such small country towns; and forests of pine and birch around her—Holmogory looks the very spot on which a poet of the people might be born!

CHAPTER II.

A Peasant Poet.

IN the grass-grown square of Archangel, between the fire-tower and the court of justice, stands a bronze figure on a round marble shaft; a figure showing a good deal of naked chest, and holding (with a Cupid's help) a lyre on the left arm. A Roman robe flows down the back. You wonder what such a figure is doing in such a place; a bit of false French art in a city of monks and trade! The man in whose name it has been raised was a poet; a poet racy of the soil; a village genius; who, among merits of many kinds, had the high quality of being a genuine Russian, and of writing in his native tongue.

For fifty years Lomonosoff was called a fool—a clever fool—for having wasted his genius on coachmen and cooks. Court ladies laughed at his whimsy of writing verses for the common herd to read; and learned dons considered him crazy for not doing all his more serious work in French. A change has come; the court speaks Russ; and society sees some merit in the phrases which it once contemned. The language of books and science is no longer foreign to the soil; and all classes of the people have the sense to read and speak in their musical and copious native speech. This happy change is due to Michael Lomonosoff, the peasant boy!

Born in this forest village on the Dvina bluffs (in 1711), he sprang from that race of free colonists who had come into the north country from Novgorod the Great. His father, Vassili Lomonosoff, a boatman, getting his bread by netting and spearing fish on the great river, brought him up among nets and boats, until the lad was big enough to slip his chain, throw down his pole, and push into the outer sea. Not many books were then to be got in a forest town like Holmogory, and some lives of saints and a Slavonic Bible were his only reading for many years. A good priest (as I learn on the spot) took notice of the child, and taught him to read the old Slavonic words. These books he got by heart; making heroes of the Hebrew prophets, and reading with ardour of his native saints. The priest soon taught him all he knew, and being a man of good heart, he sought around him for the means of sending the lad to school. But where, in those dark ages, could a school be found? He knew of schools for priests, and for the sons of priests; but schools for peasants, and for the sons of peasants, did not then exist. Could he be placed with a priest and sent to school? The village pastor wrote to a friend in Moscow, who, though poor himself,' agreed to take the lad into his house. A train of carts came through the village on its way to Moscow, carrying fur and fish for sale; and the priest arranged with the drivers that Michael should go with them, trudging at their side, and helping them on the road. At ten years old he left his forest home, and walked to the great city, a distance of nearly a thousand miles.

The priest in Moscow sent him to the clerical school, where he learned some Latin, French, and German; in all of which tongues, as well as in Russian, he afterwards spoke and wrote. He also learned to work for his living as a polisher and setter of stones. A lad who can dine off a crust of rye-bread and a cup of cabbage broth, is easily fed; and Michael, though he stuck to his craft, and lived by it, found plenty of time for the cultivation of his higher gifts. He was a good artist; for the time and place a very good artist; as the Jove-like head in the great hall of the University of Moscow proves. This head,—the poet's own gift, was executed in mosaic by his hands.

After learning all that the monks could teach him in Moscow, he left that city for Germany, where he lived some years as artist, teacher, and professor; mastering thoroughly the modern languages, and the liberal arts. When he came back to his native soil he was one of the deepest pundits of his time; a man of name and proof; respected in foreign universities for his wonderful sweep and grasp of mind. Studying many branches of science, he made himself a reputation in every branch. A Russian has a variety of gifts, and Michael was in every sense a Russ. While yet a lad it was said of him that he could mend a net, sing a ditty, drive a cart, build a cabin, and guide a boat with equal skill. When he grew up to be a man, it was said of him with no less truth, that he could at the same time crack a joke and heat a crucible; pose a logician, and criticise a poet; draw the human figure, and make a map of the stars. Coming back to Russia with such a name, he found the world at his feet; a professor's chair, with the rank of a nobleman, and the office of a councillor of state; dignities which a professor now enjoys by legal right. A strong Germanic influence met him, as a native intruder in a region of learning, closed in that age to the Russ; but he joked and pushed, and fought his way into the highest seats. He not only won a place in the Academy which Peter the Great had founded on the Neva, but in a few years he became its living soul.

Yet Michael remained a peasant and a Russian all his days. He drank a great many drams, and was never ashamed of being drunk. One day,— as the members of that Academy tell the tale—he was picked up from the gutter by one who knew him. "Hush, take care," said the good Samaritan softly; "get up quietly and come home, lest some one of the Academy should see us." "Fool!" cried the tipsy professor, "Academy? I am the Academy!"

Not without cause is this proud boast attributed to the peasant's son; for Lomonosoff was the Academy, at least on the Russian side. The breadth of his knowledge seems a marvel, even in days when a special student is expected to be an encyclopedic man, with the whole of nature for his province. He wrote in Latin and in German before he wrote in Russ. He was a miner, a physician, and a poet. He was a painter, a carver, and draughtsman. He wrote on grammar, on drugs, on music, and on the theory of ice. One of his best books is a criticism on the Varegs in Russia; one of his best papers is a treatise on microscopes and telescopes. He wrote on the Aurora Borealis, on the Duties of a Journalist, on the uses of a Barometer, and on explorations in the Polar Sea. In the records of nearly every science and art his name is found. Astronomy owes him something, chemistry something, metallurgy something. But the glory of Lomonosoff was his verse, of which he wrote a great deal, and in many different styles; lays, odes, tragedies, an unfinished epic, and moral pieces without end.

The rank of a great poet is not claimed for Michael Lomonosoff by judicious critics. No creation like Oneghin, not even like Lavretski, came from his pen. His merit lies in the fact that he was the first writer who dared to be Russian in his art. But though it is the chief, it is far from being the only distinction which Lomonosoff enjoys, even as a poet. The mechanism of literature owes to his daring a reform, of which no man now living will see the end. The Russ are a religious people, to whom phrases of devotions are as their daily bread; but the language of their Church is not the language of their streets; and their books, though calling themselves Russ, were printed in a dialect which few except their popes and the Old Believers could understand. This old dialect, Lomonosoff laid aside, and took up in its stead the fluent and racy idiom of the market and the quay. But he had a poetic music to invent, as well as a poetic idiom to adapt. The poetry of a kindred race,—the Poles—supplied him with a model, on which he built for the Russ that tonical lilt and flow, which ever since his time has been adopted by writers of verse as the most perfect vehicle for their poetic speech.

But greater than his poetic merit is the fact on which writers like Lamanski love to dwell, that Lomonosoff was a thorough Russian in his habits and ideas; and that after his election into the Academy, he set his heart upon nationalising that body, so as to render it Russian; just as the Berlin Academy was German, and the Paris Academy was French.

In his own time Lomonosoff met with little encouragement from the court. That court was German; the society nearest it was German; and German was the language of scientific thought. A Russian was a savage; and the speech of the common people was condemned to the bazaars and streets. Lomonosoff introduced that speech into literature, and into the discussions of learned men.

A statue to such a peasant marks a period in the nation's upward course. A line on the marble shaft records the fact that this figure was cast in 1829; and a second line states that it was removed in 1867 to its present site. Here, too, is progress. Forty years ago, a place behind the courts was good enough for a poet who was also a fisherman's son; even though he had done a fine thing in writing his verses in his native tongue; but thirty years later it had come to be understood by the people that no place is good enough for the man who has crowned them with his own glory; and as they see that this figure of Michael Lomonosoff is an honour to the province even more than to the poet, they have raised his pedestal in the public square.

Would that it had fallen into native hands! Modelled by a French sculptor, in the worst days of a bad school, it is a stupid travestie of truth and art. The rustics and fishermen, staring at the lyre and Cupid, at the naked shoulders and the Roman robe, wonder how their poet came to wear such a dress. This man is not the fellow whom their fathers knew; that laughing lad who laid down his tackle to become the peer of emperors and kings. Some day a native sculptor, working in the local spirit, will make a worthier monument of the peasant bard. A tall young fellow, with broad, white brow and flashing eyes, in shaggy sheep-skin wrap, broad belt, capacious boots, and high fur cap; his right hand grasping a pole and net, his left hand holding an open Bible; that would be Michael as he lived, and as men remember him now that he is dead.

Four years ago (the anniversary of his death in 1765) busts were set up, and burses founded in many colleges and schools, in honour of the peasant's son. Moscow took the lead; St. Petersburg followed; and the example spread to Harkof and Kazan. A school was built at Holmogory in the poet's name; to smooth the path of any new child of genius who may spring from this virgin soil. May it live for ever!

CHAPTER III.

Forest Scenes.

From Holgomory to Kargopol, from Kargopol to Vietegra, we pass through an empire of villages; not a single place on a road four hundred miles in length, that could by any form of courtesy be called a town. The track runs on and on, now winding by the river bank, now eating its way through the forest growths; but always flowing, as it were, in one thin line from north to south; ferrying deep rivers; dragging through shingle, slime, and peat; crashing over broken rocks; and crawling up gentle heights. His horses four abreast, and lashed to the tarantass with ropes and chains, the driver tears along the road, as though he were racing with his Chert—his Evil One; and all in the hope of getting from his thankless fare an extra cup of tea. It is the joke of a Russian jarvy, that he will "drive you out of your senses for ten kopeks." From dawn to sunset, day by day, it is one long race through bogs and pines. The landscape shows no dykes, no hedges, and no gates; no signs that tell of a personal owning of the land. We whisk by a log-fire, and a group of tramps, who flash upon us with a sullen greeting, some of them starting to their feet. "What are those fellows, Dimitri?"

"They seem to be some of the Runaways."

"Runaways! Who are the Runaways, and what are they running away from?"

"Queer fellows, who don't like work, who won't obey orders, who never rest in one place. You find them in the woods about here everywhere. They are savages. In Kargopol you can learn about them."

At the town of Kargopol, on the river Onega, in the province of Olonetz, I hear something of these Runaways, as of a troublesome and dangerous set of men, bad in themselves, and still worse as a sign. I hear of them afterwards in Novgorod the Great, and in Kazan. The community is widely spread. Timashef is aware that these unsocial bodies exist in the provinces of Yaroslav, Archangel, Vologda, Novgorod, Kostroma, and Perm.

These Runaways are vagabonds. Leaving house and land, throwing down their rights as peasants and burghers, they dress themselves in rags, assume the pilgrim's staff, retire from their families, push into forest depths, and dwell in quagmires and sandy rifts, protesting against the official Empire and the official Church. Some may lead a harmless life; the peasants helping them with food and drink; while they spend their days in dozing and their nights in prayer. Even when their resistance to the world is passive only; it is a protest hard to bear and harder still to meet. They will not labour for the things that perish. They will not bend their necks to magistrate and prince. They do not admit the law under which they live. They hold that the present imperial system is the devil's work; that the Prince of Darkness sits enthroned in the Winter Palace; that the lords and ladies who surround him are the lying witnesses and the fallen saints. Their part is not with the world, from which they fly, as Abraham fled from the Cities of the Plain.

Many of the peasants, either sympathizing with their views or fearing their vengeance, help them to support their life in the woods. No door is ever closed on them; no voice is ever raised against them. Even in the districts which they are said to ravage occasionally in search of food, hardly anything can be learned about them, least of all by the masters of police.

Fifteen months ago, the Governor of Olonetz reported to General Timashef, Minister of the Interior, that a great number of these Runaways were known to be living in his province and in the adjoining provinces, who were more or less openly supported by the peasantry in their revolt against social order and the reigning Prince. On being asked by the Minister what should be done, he hinted that nothing else would meet the evil but a seizure of vagabonds on all the roads, and in all the forest paths, in the vast countries lying north of the Volga, from Lake Ilmen to the Ural crests. His hints were taken in St. Petersburg, and hundreds of arrests were made; but whether the real Runaways were caught by the police was a question open to no less doubt than that of how to deal with them when they were caught—according to the new and liberal code.

Roused by a sense of danger, the government has been led into making inquiries far and near, the replies to which are of a kind to flutter the kindest hearts and puzzle the wisest heads. To wit:—the Governor of Kazan reports to General Timashef that he has collected proof; (1) that in his province the Runaways have a regular organization; (2) that they have secret places for meeting and worship; (3) that they have chiefs whom they obey and trust. How can a legal minister deal with cases of an aspect so completely Oriental? Is it a crime to give up house and land? Is it an offence to live in deserts and lonely caves? What article in the civil code prevents a man from living like Seraphim in a desert; like Philaret the Less, in a grave-yard? Yet, on the other side, how can a reforming Emperor suffer his people to fall back into the nomadic state? A Runaway is not a weakness only, but a peril; since the spirit of his revolt against social order is precisely that which the reformers have most cause to dread. In going back from his country, he is going back into chaos.

The mighty drama now proceeding in his country, turns on the question raised by the Runaway. Can the Russian peasant live under law? If it shall prove on trial that any large portion of the Russian peasantry shares this passion for a vagabond life— as some folk hope, and still more fear—the Great Experiment will fail, and civil freedom will be lost for a hundred years.

The facts collected by the minister have been laid before a special committee, named by the

Crown. That committee is now sitting; but no conclusion has yet been reached, and no suggestion for meeting the evil can be pointed out.

Village after village passes to the rear! Russ hamlets are so closely modelled on a common type, that when you have seen one, you have seen a host; when you have seen two, you have seen the whole. Your sample may be either large or small, either log-built or mud-built, either hidden in forest or exposed on steppe; yet in the thousands on thousands to come, you will observe no change in the prevailing forms. There is a Great Russ hamlet and a Little Russ hamlet; one with its centre in Moscow, as the capital of Great Russia; the second with its centre in Kief, the capital of Little Russia.

A Great Russ village consists of two lines of cabins parted from each other by a wide and dirty lane. Each homestead stands alone. From ten to a hundred cabins make a village. Built of the same pine-logs, notched and bound together, each house is like its fellow, except in size. The Elder's hut is bigger than the rest; and after the Elder's house comes the whisky-shop. Four squat walls, two tiers in height, and pierced by doors and windows; such is the shell. The floor is mud, the shingle deal. The walls are rough, the crannies stuffed with moss. No paint is used, and the log fronts soon become grimy with rain and smoke. The space between each hut lies open and unfenced; a slough of mud and mire, in which the pigs grunt and wallow, and the wolf-dogs snarl and fight. The lane is planked. One house here and there may have a balcony, a cow-shed, an upper story. Near the hamlet rises a chapel built of logs, and roofed with plank; but here you find a flush of colour, if not a gleam of gold. The walls of the chapel are sure to be painted white, the roof is sure to be painted green. Some wealthy peasant may have gilt the cross.

Beyond these dreary cabins lie the still more dreary fields, which the people till. Flat, unfenced, and lowly, they have nothing of the poetry of our fields in the Suffolk and Essex plains; no hedgerow ferns, no clumps of fruit trees, and no hints of home. The patches set apart for kitchen-stuff are not like gardens even of their homely kind; they look like workhouse plots of space laid out by yard and rule, in which no living soul had any part. These patches are always mean, and you search in vain for such a dainty as a flower.

Among the Little Russ—in the old Polish circles of the south and west, you see a village group of another kind. Instead of the grimy logs, you have a predominant mixture of green and white; instead of the formal blocks, you have a scatter of cottages in the midst of trees. The cabins are built of earth and reeds; the roof is thatched with straw; and the walls of the homestead are washed with lime. A fence of mats and thorns runs round the group. If every house appears to be small, it stands in a yard and garden of its own. The village has no streets. Two, and only two, openings pierce the outer fence; one north, one south; and in feeling your way from one opening in the fence to another, you push through a maze of lanes between reeds and spines, beset by savage dogs. Each new-comer would seem to have pitched his tent where he pleased; taking care to cover his hut and yard by the common fence.

A village built without a plan, in which every house is surrounded by a garden, covers an immense extent of ground. Some of the Kozak villages are as widely spread as towns. Of course there is a church, with its glow of colour and poetic charm.

From Kief on the Dnieper to Kalatch on the Don, you find the villages of this second type. The points of difference lie in the house and in the garden; and must spring from difference of education, if not of race. The Great Russians are of a timid, soft, and fluent type. They like to huddle in a crowd, to club their means, to live under a common roof, and stand or fall by the family tree. The Little Russians are of a quick, adventurous and hardy type; who like to stand apart, each for himself, with scope and range enough for the play of all his powers. A Great Russian carries his bride to his father's shed; a Little Russian carries her to a cabin of his own.

The forest melts and melts! We meet a woman driving in a cart alone; a girl darts past us in the mail; anon we come upon a waggon, guarded by troops on foot, containing prisoners, partly chained, in charge of an ancient dame.

This service of the road is due from village to

village; and on a party of travellers coming into a hamlet, the Elder must provide for them the things required—carts, horses, drivers—in accordance with their podorojna; but in many villages the party finds no men, or none except the very young and the very old. Husbands are leagues away; fishing in the Polar Seas, cutting timber in the Kargopol forests, trapping fox and beaver in the Ural Mountains; leaving their wives alone for months. These female villages are curious things, in which a man of pleasant manners may find a chance of flirting to his heart's content.

Villages, more villages, yet more villages! We pass a gang of soldiers marching by the side of a peasant's cart, in which lies a prisoner, chained; we spy a wolf in the copse; we meet a pilgrim on his way to Solovetsk; we come upon a gang of boys whose clothes appear to be out at wash; we pass a broken waggon; we start at the howl of some village dogs; and then go winding forward hour by hour, through the silent woods. Some touch of grace and poetry charms our eyes in the most desolate scenes. A virgin freshness crisps and shakes the leaves. The air is pure. If nearly all the lines are level, the sky is blue, the sunshine gold. Many of the trees are rich with amber, pink and brown; and every vagrant breeze makes music in the pines. A peasant and his dog troop past, reminding me of scenes in Kent. A convent here and there peeps out. A patch of forest is on fire, from the burning mass of which a tongue of pale pink flame laps out and up through a pall of purple smoke. A clearing, swept by some former fire, is all aglow with autumnal flowers. A bright beck dashes through the falling leaves. A comely child, with flaxen curls and innocent northern eyes, stands bowing in the road, with an almost Syrian grace. A woman comes up with a bowl of milk. A group of girls are washing at a stream, under the care of either the Virgin Mother or some local saint. On every point, the folk, if homely, are devotional and polite; brightening their forest breaks with chapel and cross, and making their dreary road, as it were, a path of light towards heaven.

We dash into a village near a small black lake.

CHAPTER IV.

Patriarchal Life.

"No horses to be got till night!"

"You see," smirks the village Elder, "we are making holiday; it is a bridal afternoon, and the Patriarch gives a feast on account of Vanka's nuptials with Nadia."

"Nadia! Well, a pretty name. We shall have horses in the evening, eh? Then let it be so. Who are yon people? Ha! the church! Come, let us follow them, and see the crowning. Is this Vanka a fine young fellow?"

"Vanka! yes; in the bud. He is a lad of seventeen years; said to be eighteen years—the legal age—but, hem! He counts for nothing in the match."

"Why, then, is he going to take a wife?"

"Hem! that is the Patriarch's business. Daniel wants some help in the house. Old Dan, you see, is Vanka's father, and the poor old motherkin has been worn by him to the skin and bone. She is ten years older than he, and the Patriarch wants a younger woman at his beck and call; a woman to milk his cow, to warm his stove, and to make his tea."

"He wants a good servant?"

"Yes; he wants a good servant, and he will get one in Nadia."

"Then this affair is not a love-match?"

"Much as most. The lad, though young, is said to have been in love; for lads are silly and girls are sly; but he is not in love with the woman whom his father chooses for him."

"One of your village girls?"

"Yes, Lousha; a pretty minx, with round blue eyes and pouting lips; and not a ruble in the world. Now, Nadia has five brass samovars and fifteen silver spoons. The heart of Daniel melted towards those fifteen silver spoons."

"And what says Vanka to the match?"

"Nothing. What can he say? The Patriarch has done it all: tested the spoons, accepted the bride, arranged the feast, and fixed the day."

"Russia is the land for you fathers, eh?"

"Each in his time; the father first, the offspring next. Each in his day; the boy will be a Patriarch in his turn. A son is nobody till his parent dies."

"Not in such an affair as choosing his own wife?"

"No; least of all in choosing his own wife. You see our ways are old and homely, like the Bible ways. A Patriarch rules under every roof—not only lives but rules; and where in the patriarchal times do you read that the young men went out into the world and chose them partners for themselves? Our Patriarch settles such things; he and the Proposeress."

"Proposeress! Pray what is a Proposeress?"

"An ancient crone, who lives in yon cabin, near the bridge; a poor old waif, who feeds upon her craft, who tells your fortune by a card, who acts as agent for the girls, and is feared by everybody as a witch."

"Have you such a Proposeress in every village?"

"Not in every one. Some villages are too poor, for these old women must be paid in good kopeks. The craftier sisters live in towns, where they can tell you a good deal more. These city witches can rule the planets, while the village witches can only rule the cards."

"You really think they rule the planets?"

"Who can tell? We see they rule the men and women; yet every man has his planet and his angel. You must know, the girls who go to the Proposeress leave with her a list of what they have—so many samovars, so much linen and household stuff. It is not often they have silver spoons. These lists the patriarchs come to her house and read. A sly fellow, like Old Dan, will steal to her door at dusk, when no one is about, and putting down his flask of whisky on the table, ask the old crone to drink. 'Come, motherkin,' he will giggle, 'bring out your list, and let us talk it over.' 'What are you seeking, Father Daniel?' leers the crone. 'A wife for Vanka, motherkin, a wife! Here, take a drink; the dram will do you good; and now bring out your book. A fine stout lass, with plenty of sticks and stones for me!' 'Ha!' pouts the witch, her finger on the glass, 'you want to see my book! Well, fatherkin, I have two nice lasses on my hands,—good girls, and well-to-do; either one or other just the bride for Vanka. Here, now, is Lousha; pretty thing, but no household stuff; blue eyes, but not yet twenty; teeth like pearls, but shaky on her feet. Not do for you and your son? Why not? Well, as you please; I show my wares, you take them or you leave them. Lousha is a dainty thing—you need not blow the shingles off! Come, come, there's Dounia; well-built, buxom lassie; never raised a scandal in her life; had but one lover, a neighbour's boy. What sticks and stones? Dounia is a prize in herself,—she eats very little, and she works like a horse. She has four samovars (Russian tea-urns). Not do for you! Well, now you *are* in luck to-night, little father. Here's Nadia!'—on which comes out the story of her samovars and her silver spoons."

"And so the match is made?"

"A fee is paid to the parish priest, a day for the rite is fixed, and all is over,—except the feast, the drinking, and the headache."

"Tell me about Nadia?"

"You think Nadia such a pretty name. For my part, I prefer Marfousha. My wife was Marfa; called Marfousha when the woman is a pet."

"Is Nadia young and fair?"

"Young? Twenty-nine. Fair? Brown as a turf."

"Twenty-nine, and Vanka seventeen!"

"But she is big and bony; strong as a mule, and she can go all day on very little food."

"All that would be well enough if what you wanted was a slave to thrust a spade and drive a cart."

"That is what the Patriarch wants; a servant for himself, a partner for his boy."

"How came Vanka to accept her?"

"Daniel shows him her silver spoons, her shining urns, and her chest of household stuff. The lad stares wistfully at these fine things; Lousha is absent, and the old man nods. The woman kisses him, and all is done."

"Poor Lousha! where is she to-day?"

"Left in the fields to grow. She is not strong enough yet to marry. She could not work for her husband and her husband's father as a wife must do. Far better wait awhile. At twenty-nine she will be big and bony like Nadia; then she will be fit to marry, for then her wild young spirits will be gone."

We walk along the plank-road from the station to the church; which is crowded with men and women in their holiday attire; the girls in red skirts and bodices, trimmed with fur, and even with silver lace; the men in clean capotes and round fur caps, with golden tassels and scarlet tops. The rite is nearly over; the priest has joined the pair in holy matrimony; and the bride and groom come forth, arrayed in their tinsel crowns. The King leads out the Queen, who certainly looks old enough to be his dam. One hears so much about marital rights in Russia, and the claim of women to be thrashed in evidence of their husbands' love, that one can hardly help wondering how long it will be before Vanka can beat his wife. Not at present, clearly; so that one would feel some doubt of their "sober certainty of bliss," except for our knowledge that if Vanka fails, the Patriarch will not scruple to use his whip.

Crowned with her rim of gilt brass, the bony bride, in stiff brocade and looking her fifteen silver spoons, slides down the sloppy lane to her future home.

The whisky-shops—we have two in our village for the comfort of eighty or ninety souls—are loud and busy, pouring out nips and nippets of their liquid death. Fat, bearded men are hugging and kissing each other in their pots, while the younger fry of lads and lassés wend in demure and pensive silence to an open ground, where they mean to wind up the day's festivities with a dance. This frolic is a thing to see. A ring of villagers, old and young, get ready to applaud the sport. The dancers stand apart; a knot of young men here, a knot of maidens there, each sex by itself, and silent as a crowd of mutes. A piper breaks into a tune; a youth pulls off his cap, and challenges his girl with a wave and bow. If the girl is willing, she waves her handkerchief in token of assent; the youth advances, takes a corner of the kerchief in his hand, and leads his lassie round and round. No word is spoken, and no laugh is heard. Stiff with cords and rich with braid, the girl moves heavily by herself, going round and round, and never allowing her partner to touch her hand. The pipe goes droning on for hours in the same sad key and measure; and the prize of merit in this "circling," as the dance is called, is given by spectators to the lassie who in all that summer revelry has never spoken and never smiled!

Men chat with men, and laugh with men; but if they approach the women, they are speechless; making signs with their caps only; and their dumb appeal is answered by a wave of the kerchief—answered without words. These romps go on till bedtime; when the men, being warm with drink, if not with love, begin to reel and shout like Comus and his tipsy crew.

The Patriarch stops at home, delighted to spend his evening with Nadia and her silver spoons.

Even when her husband is a grown-up man, a woman has to come under the common roof, and live by the common rule. If she would like to get her share of the cabbage soup and the buckwheat pudding, not to speak of a new bodice now and then, she must contrive to please the old man, and she can only please him by doing at once whatever he bids her do. The Greek church knows of no divorce; and once married, you are tied for life; but neither party has imagination enough to be wretched in his lot, unless the beans should fail or the Patriarch lay on the whip.

"Would not a husband protect his wife?"

"No," says the Elder, "not where his father is concerned."

A Patriarch is lord in his own house and family, and no man has a right to interfere with him; not even the village Elder and the imperial Judge. He stands above oral and written law. His cabin is not only a castle, but a church, and every act of his done within that cabin is supposed to be private and divine.

"If a woman flew to her husband from blows and stripes?"

"The husband must submit. What would you have? Two wills under one roof? The shingles would fly off."

"The young men always yield?"

"What should they do but yield? Is not old age to be revered? Is not experience good? Can a man have lived his life and not learned wisdom with his years? Now, it is said, the fashion is about to change; the young men are to rule the house; the patriarchs are to hide their beards. But not in my time; not in my time!"

"Do the women readily submit to what the Patriarch says?"

"They must. Suppose Nadia beaten by Old Dan. She comes to me with her shoulders black and blue. I call a meeting of patriarchs to hear her tale. What comes of it? She tells them her father beats her. She shows her scars. The patriarchs ask her why he beats her? She owns that she refused to do this or that, as he bade her; something, it may be, which he ought not to have asked, and she ought not to have done; but the principle of authority is felt to be at stake; for, if a Patriarch is not to rule his house, how is the Elder to rule his village, the Governor his province, the Tsar his empire? All authorities stand or fall together; and the patriarchs find that the woman is a fool, and that a second drubbing will do her good."

"They would not order her to be flogged?"

"Not now; the new law forbids it; that is to say, in public. In his own cabin Daniel may flog Nadia when he likes."

This "new law" against flogging women in public is an edict of the present reign; a part of that mighty scheme of social reform which the Emperor is carrying out on every side. It is not popular in the village, since it interferes with the rights of men, and cripples the patriarchs in dealing with the defenceless sex. Since this edict put an end to the open flogging of women, the men have been forced to invent new modes of punishing their wives, and their sons' wives, since they fancy that a private beating does but little good, because it carries no sting of shame. A news-sheet gives the following as a sample: Euphrosine M——, a peasant woman living in the province of Kherson, is accused by her husband of unfaithfulness to her vows. The rustic calls a meeting of patriarchs, who hear his story, and without hearing the wife in her defence, condemn her to be walked through the village stark naked, in broad daylight, in the presence of all her friends. That sentence is executed on a frosty day. Her guilt is never proved; yet she has no appeal from the decision of that village court!

A village is an original and separate power; in every sense a state within the state.

CHAPTER V.

Village Republics.

A VILLAGE is a republic, governed by a law, a custom, and a ruler of its own.

In Western Europe and the United States a hamlet is no more than a little town in which certain gentlefolk, farmers, tradesmen, and their dependants dwell; people who are as free to go away, as they were free to come. A Russian village is not a small town, with this mixture of ranks, but a collection of cabins, tenanted by men of one class, and one calling; men who have no power to quit the fields they sow; who have to stand and fall by each other; who hold their lands under a common bond; who pay their taxes in a common sum; who give up their sons as soldiers in the common name.

These Village Republics are confined in practice to Great Russia, and the genuine Russ. In Finland, in the Baltic provinces, they are unknown; in Astrakhan, Siberia, and Kazan, they are unknown; in Kief, Podolia, and the Ukraine Steppe, they are unknown; in the Georgian highlands, in the Circassian valleys, on the Ural slopes, they are equally unknown. In fact, the existence of these peasant Republics in a province, is the first and safest test of nationality. Wherever they are found, the soil is Russian, and the people Russ.

The provinces over which they spread are many in number, vast in extent, and rich in patriotic virtue. They extend from the walls of Smolensk to the neighbourhood of Viatka; from the Gulf of Onega to the Kozak settlements on the Don. They cover an empire fifteen or sixteen times as large as France; the empire of Ivan the Terrible; that Russia which lay around the four ancient capitals—Novgorod, Vladimir, Moscow, Pskoff.

What is a Village Republic?

Is it Arcady, Utopia, New Jerusalem, Brook Farm, Oneida Creek, Abode of Love? Not one of these societies can boast of more than a passing resemblance to a Russian commune.

A Village Republic is an association of peasants, living like a body of monks and nuns in a convent; living on lands of their own, protected by chiefs of their own, and ruled by customs of their own; but here the analogy between a commune and a convent ends; for a peasant marries, multiplies, and fills the earth. It is an agricultural family, holding an estate in hand like a Shaker Union; but instead of flying from the world and having no friendship beyond the village bounds, they knit their interests up, by marrying with those of the adjacent communes. It is an association of laymen like a phalanx; but instead of dividing the harvest, they divide the land; and that division having taken place, their rule is for every man to do the best he can for himself, without regard to his brother's needs. It is a working company, in which the field and forest belong to all the partners in equal shares, as in a

Gaelic clan and a Celtic sept; but the Russian rustic differs from a Highland chiel, and an Irish kerne, in owning no hereditary chief. It is a socialistic group, with property,—the most solid and lasting property—in common, like the Bible votaries at Oneida Creek; but these partners in the soil never dream of sharing their goods and wives. It is a tribal unit, holding what it owns under a common obligation, like a Jewish house; but the associates differ from a Jewish house in bearing different names, and not affecting unity of blood.

By seeing what a Village Republic is not, we gain some insight into what it is.

We find some sixty or eighty men of the same class, with the same pursuits; who have consented, they and their fathers for them, to stay in one spot; to build a hamlet; to elect an Elder with unusual powers; to hold their land in general, not in several; and to dwell in cabins near each other, face to face. The purpose of their association is mutual help.

A pack of wolves may have been the founders of the first Village Republic. Even now, when the forests are thinner, and the villages stronger than of yore, the cry of "Wolf" is no welcome sound; and when the frost is keen, the village homesteads have to be watched in turns, by day and night. A wolf in the Russian forests is like a Red-skin on the Kansas plains. The strength of a party led by an Elder, fighting in defence of a common home, having once been proved by success against wolves, it would be easy to rouse that strength against the fox and the bear, the vagabond and the thief. In a region full of forests, lakes, and bogs, a lonely settler has no chance, and Russia is even yet a country of forests, ·lakes, and bogs. The settlers must club their means and powers, and bind themselves to stand by each other in weal and woe. Wild beasts are not their only foes. A fall of snow is worse than a raid of wolves; for the snow may bury their sheds, destroy their roads, imprison them in tombs, from which a single man would never be able to fight his way. The wolves are now driven into the woods, but the snow can never be beaten back into the sky; and while the Northern storms go raging on, a peasant who tills the Northern soil will need for his protection an enduring social bond.

These peasant republicans find this bond of union in the soil. They own the soil in common, not each in his own right, but every one in the name of all. They own it for ever, and in equal shares. A man and his wife make the social unit, recognised by the commune as a house, and every house has a claim to a fair division of the family estate; to so much field, to so much wood, to so much kitchen ground, as that estate will yield to each. Once in three years all claims fall in, all holdings cease, a fresh division of the land is made. A commune being a republic, and the men all peers, each voice must be heard in council, and every claim must be considered in parcelling the estate. The whole is parted into as many lots as there are married couples in the village; so much arable, so much forest, so much cabbage-bed for each. Goodness of soil and distance from the home are set against each other in every case.

But the principle of association passes, like the needs out of which it springs, beyond the village bounds. Eight or ten communes join themselves into a Canton (a sort of parish); ten or twelve cantons form a Volost (a sort of hundred). Each circle is self-governed; in fact, a local republic.

From ancient times, the members of these village democracies derive a body of local rights; of kin to those family rights which reforming ministers and judges think it wiser to leave alone. They choose their own elders, hold their own courts, inflict their own fines. They have a right to call meetings, draw up motions, and debate their communal affairs. They have authority over all their members, whether these are rich or poor. They can depose their elders, and set up others in their stead. A peasant republic is a patriarchal circle, exercising powers which the Emperor has not given, and dares not take away.

The Elder, (called in Russian Starosta) is the village chief.

The Elder is elected by the peasants from their own body; elected for three years; though he is seldom changed at the end of his term; and men have been known to serve their neighbours in this office from the age of forty until they died. Every one is qualified for the post; though it seldom falls, in practice, to a man who is either unable or unwilling to pay for drink. The rule is, for the richest peasant of the village to be chosen, and a stranger driving into a hamlet in search of the Elder will not often be wrong in pulling up his tarantass at the biggest door. These peasants meet in a chapel, in a barn, in a dram-shop, as the case may be; they whisper to each other their selected name; they raise a loud shout and a clatter of horny hands; and when the man of their choice has bowed his head, accepting their vote, they sally to a drinking-shop, where they shake hands and kiss each other over nippets of whisky and jorums of quass. An unpaid servant of his village, the Russian Elder, like an Arab Sheikh, is held accountable for everything that happens to go wrong. Let the summer be hot, let the winter be dure, let the crop be scant, let the whisky be thin, let the roads be unsafe, let the wolves be out —the Elder is always the man to blame. Sometimes, not often, a rich peasant tries to shirk this office, as a London banker shuns the dignity of lord mayor. But such a man, if he escape, will not escape scot free. A Commune claims the service of her members, and no one can avoid her call without suffering a fine in either meal or malt. The man who wishes to escape election has to smirk and smile like the man who wishes to win the prize. He has to court his neighbours in the grog-shop, in the church, and in the field; flattering their weakness, treating them to drink, and whispering in their ear that he is either too young, too old, or too busy for the office they would thrust upon him. When the time comes round for a choice to be made, the villagers pass him by with winks and shrugs, expecting, when the day is over, to have one more chance of drinking at his expense.

An Elder chosen by this village parliament is clothed with strange, unclassified powers; for he is mayor and sheikh in one; a personage known to the law, as well as a patriarch clothed with domestic rights. Some of his functions lie beyond the law, and clash with articles in the imperial code.

To wit: an Elder sitting in his village court retains the power to beat and flog. No one else in Russia, from the lord on his lawn and the general on parade, down to the merchant in his shop and the rider on a sledge, can lawfully strike his man. By one wise stroke of his pen, the Emperor made all men equal before the stick; and breaches of this rule are judged with such wholesome zeal, that the savage energy of the upper ranks is completely checked. Once only have I seen a man beat another —an officer who pushed and struck a soldier, to prevent him getting entangled in floes of ice. But a village Elder, backed by his meeting, can defeat the imperial will, and set the beneficent public code aside.

A majority of peasants, meeting in a barn, or even in a whisky-shop, can fine and flog their fellows beyond appeal. Some rights have been taken from these village republicans in recent years; they are not allowed, as in former times, to lay the lash on women; and though they can sentence a man to twenty blows, they may not club him to death. Yet two-thirds of a village mob, in which every voter may be drunk, can pass a vote which may have the effect of sending a man to Siberia for his term of life!

CHAPTER VI.

Communism.

SUCH cases of village justice are not rare. Should a man have the misfortune, from any cause, to make himself odious to his neighbours, they can "cry a meeting," summon him to appear, and find him worthy to be expelled. They can send for the police, give the expelled member into custody, and send him up to the nearest district town. He is now a waif and stray. Rejected from his Commune, he has no place in society; he cannot live in a town, he cannot enter a village; he is simply a vagabond and an outcast, living beyond the pale of human law. The provincial governor can do little for him, even if he be minded to do anything at all. He has no means of forcing the Commune to receive him back; in fact, he has no choice, beyond that of sending such a waif to either the army or the public works. If all the forms have been observed, the village judgment is final, and the man expelled from it by such a note, is pretty sure of passing the remainder of his days on earth in either a Circassian regiment or a Siberian mine.

In the more serious cases dealt with by courts of law, a Commune has the power of reviewing the sentence passed, and even of setting it aside.

Some lout (say) is suspected of setting a barn

on fire. Seized by his Elder and given in charge to the police, he is carried up to the assize town, where he is tried for his alleged offence, and after proof being given on either side, he is acquitted by the jury and discharged by the judge. It might be fancied that such a man would return to his cabin and his field, protected by the courts. But no; the Commune, which has done him so much wrong already, may complete the injury by refusing to receive him back. A meeting may review the jurors and the judge, decline their verdict, try the man once more in secret, and condemn him, in his absence, to the loss—not simply of his house and land—but of his fame and caste.

The Communes have other, and not less curious, rights. No member of a Commune can quit his village without the general leave, without a passport signed by the Elder, who can call him home without giving reasons for his acts. The absent brother must obey, on penalty of being expelled from his Commune: that is to say—in a Russian village, as in an Indian caste—being flung out of organized society into infinite space.

Nor can the absent member escape from this tribunal by forfeiting his personal rights. An Elder grants him leave to travel in very rare cases, and for very short terms; often for a month, now and then a quarter, never for more than a year. That term, whether long or short, is the limit of a man's freedom; when it expires, he must return to his Commune, under penalty of seizure by the police as a vagabond living without a pass.

A village parliament is holden once a-year, when every holder of house and field has the right to be heard. The suffrage is general, the voting by ballot. Any member can bring up a motion, which the Elder is compelled to put. An unpopular Elder may be deposed, and some one else elected in his stead. Subjects of contention are not lacking in these peasant parliaments; but the fiercest battles are those fought over roads, imperial taxes, conscripts, wood-rights, water-rights, whisky licenses, and the choice of lots.

What may be termed the external affairs of the village—highways, fisheries, and forest-rights—are settled, not with imperial officers, but with their neighbours of the Canton and the Volost. The Canton and the Volost treat with the general, governor and police. A minister looks for what he needs to the association, not to the separate members; and when rates are levied and men are wanted, the Canton and the Volost receive their orders and proceed to raise alike the money and the men. The Crown has only to send out orders; and the money is paid, the men are raised. A system so effective and so cheap, is a convenience to the ministers of finance and war so great, that the haughtiest despots, and the wisest reformers, have not dared to touch the interior life of these peasant commonwealths.

Thus the village system remains a thing apart, not only from the outer world, but from the neighbouring town. The men who live in these sheds, who plough these fields, who angle in this lake, are living by an underived and original light. Their law is an oral law, their charter bears no seal, their franchise knows no date. They vote their own taxes, and they frame their own rules. Except in crimes of serious dye, they act as an independent court. They fine, they punish, they expel, they send unpopular men to Siberia; and even call up the civil arm in execution of their will.

Friends of these rustic republics urge as merits, in the village system, that the men are peers, that public opinion governs, that no one is exempt from the general law, that rich men find no privilege in their wealth. All this sounds well in words; and probably in seven or eight cases out of ten the peasants treat their brethren fairly; though it will not be denied that in the other two or three cases gross and comical burlesques of justice may be seen. I hear of a man being flogged for writing a paragraph in a local paper, which half, at least, of his judges could not read. Still worse, and still more flagrant, is the abuse of extorting money from the rich. A charge is made, a meeting cried, and evidence heard. If the offender falls on his knees, admits his guilt, and offers to pay a fine, the charge is dropped. The whole party marches to the whisky-shop, and spends the fine in drams. Now the villagers know pretty well the brother who is rich enough to give his rubles in place of baring his back; and when they thirst for a dram at some other man's cost, they have only to get up some flimsy charge on which that yielding brother can be tried. The man is sure to buy himself off. Then comes the farce of charge and proof, admission and fine; followed by the drinking-bout, in which from policy the offender joins;

until the virtuous villagers, warm with the fiery demon, kiss and slobber upon each other's beards, and darkness covers them up in their drunken sleep.

In Moscow, I know a man, a clerk, a thrifty fellow, born in the province of Tamboff, who has saved some money, and the fact coming out, he has been thrice called home to his village, thrice accused of trumpery offences, thrice corrected by a fine. In every case, the man was sentenced to be flogged; and he paid his money, as they knew he would, to escape from suffering and disgrace. His fines were instantly spent in drink.' A member of a village republic who has prospered by his thrift and genius finds no way of guarding himself from such assaults, except by craftily lending sums of money to the heads of houses, so as to get the leading men completely into his power.

In spite of some patent virtues, a rural system which compels the more enterprising and successful men to take up such a position against their fellows in actual self-defence, can hardly be said to serve the higher purposes for which societies exist.

These village republics are an open question; one about which there is daily strife in every office of Government, in every organ of the press. Men who differ on every other point agree in praising the rural Communes. Men who agree on every other point, part company on the merits and vices of the rural Communes.

Not a few of the ablest reformers wish to see them thrive; Royalists, like Samarin and Cherkaski, and Republicans, like Herzen and Ogareff, see in these village societies the germs of a new civilisation for East and West. Men of science, like Valuef, Bungay, and Besobrazof, on the contrary, find in these Communes nothing but evil, nothing but a legacy from the dark ages, which must pass away as the light of personal freedom dawns.

That the village Communes have some virtues may be safely said. A minister of war and a minister of finance are keenly alive to these virtues, since a man who wishes to levy troops and taxes in a quick, uncostly fashion, finds it easier to deal with fifty thousand elders, than with fifty million peasants. A minister of justice thinks with comfort of the host of watchful, unpaid eyes that are kept in self-defence on such as are suspected of falling into evil ways. These virtues are not all, not nearly all. A rural system, in which every married man has a stake in the soil, produces a conservative and pacific people. No race on earth either clings to old ways, or prays for peace so fervently, as the Russ. Where each man is a landholder, abject poverty is unknown; and Russia has scant need for poor-laws and work-houses, since she has no such misery in her midst as a permanent pauper class. Everybody has a cabin, a field, a cow; perhaps a horse and cart. Even when a fellow is lazy enough, and base enough, to ruin himself, he cannot ruin his sons. They hold their place in the Commune, as peers of all; and when they grow up to man's estate, they will obtain their lots, and set up life on their own account. The bad man dies, and leaves to his province no legacy of poverty and crime. The Communes cherish love for parents, and respect for age. They keep alive the feeling of brotherhood and equality, and inspire the country with a sentiment of mutual dependence and mutual help.

On the other side, they foster a parish spirit, tend to separate village from town, strengthen the ideas of class and caste, and favour that worst delusion in a country—of there being a state within the state! Living in his own republic, a peasant is apt to consider the burgher as a stranger living under a different and inferior rule. A peasant hears little of the Civil Code, except in his relations with the townsfolk; and he learns to despise the men who are bound by the letter of that Civil Code. Between his own institutions and those of his burgher neighbours, there is a chasm, like that which separates America from France.

CHAPTER VII.

Towns.

A TOWN is a community lying beyond the canton and volost, in which people live by burgher right and not by communal law. Unlike the peasant, a burgher has power to buy and sell, to make and mend, to enter crafts and guilds; but he is chained to his trade very much as the rustic is chained to his field. His house is built of logs, his roads are laid with planks; but then his house is painted green or pink, and his road is wide and properly laid out. In place of a free local government, the town finds a master in the minister, in the governor, in the chief of police. While the village is a separate republic, the town is a parcel of the empire; and as parcel of the empire it must follow the imperial code.

Saving the great cities, not above five or six in number, all Russian towns have a common character, and when you have seen two or three in different parts of the empire, you have seen them all. Take any river-side town of the second class (and most of these towns are built on the banks of streams) from Onega to Rostoff, from Nijni to Kremenchug. A fire-tower, a jail, a fish-market, a bazaar, and a cathedral, catch the eye at once. Above and below the town you see monastic piles. A bridge of boats connects the two banks, and a poorer suburb lies before the town. The port is crowded with smacks and rafts; the smacks bringing fish, the rafts bringing pines. What swarms of people on the wharf! How grave, how dirty, and how pinched, they look! Their sadness comes of the climate, and their dirt is of the East. "Yes, yes!" you may hear a mujik say to his fellow, speaking of some neighbour, "he is a respectable man—quite; he has a clean shirt once a-week." The rustic eats but little flesh; his dinner, even on days that are not kept as fasts, being a slice of black bread, a girkin, and a piece of dried cod. Just watch them, how they higgle for a kopek! A Russ craftsman is a fellow to deal with; ever hopeful and acquiescent; ready to please in word and act; but you are never sure that he will keep his word. He has hardly any sense of time and space. To him one hour of the day is like another, and if he has promised to make you a coat by ten in the morning, he cannot be got to see the wrong of sending it home by eleven at night.

The market reeks with oil and salt, with vinegar and fruit, with the refuse of halibut, cod, and sprats. The chief articles of sale are rings of bread, salt, girkins, pottery, tin plates, iron nails, and images of saints. The street is paved with pools, in which lie a few rough stones, to help you in stepping from stall to stall. To walk is an effort; to walk with clean feet a miracle. Such filth is too deep for shoes.

A fish-wife is of either sex; and even when she

belongs of right to the better side of human nature, she is not easy to distinguish from her lord by anything in her face and garb. Seeing her in the sharp wind, quilted in her sheep-skin coat, and legged in her deer-skin hose, her features pinched by frost, her hands blackened by toil, it would be hard to say which was the female and which the male, if Providence had not blessed the men with beards. By these two signs a Russ may be known from all other men; by his beard and by his boots; but since many of his female folk wear boots, he is only to be safely known from his partner in life by the bunch of hair upon his chin.

In the bazaar stand the shops; dark holes in the wall, like the old Moorish shops in Seville and Granada; in which the dealer stand before his counter and shows you his poor assortment of prints and stuffs, his pots and pans, his saints, his candles, and his packs of cards. Next to rye-bread and salt-fish, saints and cards are the articles mostly bought and sold; for in Russia everybody prays and plays; the noble in his club, the dealer at his shop, the boatman on his barge, the pilgrim by his wayside cross. The propensities to pray and gamble may be traced to a common root; a kind of moral fetichism, a trust in the grace of things unseen, in the merit of dead men, and even in the power of chance. A Russian takes, like a child, to every strange thing, and prides himself on the completeness of his faith. When he is not kneeling to his angel, nothing renders him so happy as the sight of a pack of cards.

Nearly everyone plays high for his means; and nothing is more common than for a burgher to stake and lose, first his money, then his boots, his cap, his caftan, every scrap of his garments, down to his very shirt. Whisky excepted, nothing drives a Russian to the devil so quickly as a pack of cards.

But see, these gamblers throw down their cards, unbonnet their heads, and fall upon their knees. The priest is coming down the street with his sacred picture and his cross. It is market-day in the town, and he is going to open and bless some shop in the bazaar; and fellows who were gambling for their shirts are now upon their knees in prayer.

The rite by which a shop, a shed, a house, is dedicated to God is not without touches of poetic beauty. Notice must be given aforetime to the parish priest, who fixes the hour of consecration, so that a man's kinsfolk and neighbours may be present, if they like. The time having come, the priest takes down his cross from the altar, a boy lights the embers in his censer; and preceded by his reader and deacon, the pope moves down the streets through crowds of kneeling men and women, most of whom rise and follow in his wake, only too eager to catch so easily and cheaply some of the celestial fire.

Entering the shop or house, the pope first purges the room by prayer, then blesses the tenant or dweller, and lastly sanctifies the place by hanging in the "corner of honour" an image of the dealer's guardian angel, so that in the time to come no act can be done in that house or shop, except under the eyes of its patron saint.

Though poor as art, such icons, placed in rooms, have power upon men's minds. Not far from Tamboff lived an old lady who was more than commonly hard upon her serfs, until the poor wretches, maddened by her use of the whip and the black hole, broke into her room at night, some dozen men, and told her, with a sudden brevity, that her hour had come and she must die. Springing from her bed, she snatched her image from the wall, and held it out against her assailants, daring them to strike the Mother of God. Dropping their clubs, they fled from before her face. Taking courage from her victory, she hung up the picture, drew on her wrapper, and followed her serfs into the yard, where, seeing that she was unprotected by her image, they set upon her with a shout, and clubbed her instantly to death.

In driving through the town we note how many are the dram shops, and how many the tipsy men. Among the smaller reforms under which the burgher has now to live is that of a thinner drink. The Emperor has put water into the whisky, and reduced the price from fifteen kopeks a glass to five. The change it not much relished by the topers, who call their thin potation "dechofka"—cheap stuff; but simpler souls give thanks to the reformer for his boon, saying, "Is he not good—our Tsar—in giving us three glasses of whisky for the price of a single glass!" Yet, thin as it is, a nippet of the fiery spirit throws a sinner off his legs, for his stomach is empty, his nerves are lax, and his blood is poor. If he were better fed he would crave less drink. Happily a Russian is not quarrelsome in his cups; he sings, and smiles, and wishes to hug you in the public street. No richer comedy is seen on any stage than that presented by two tipsy mujiks riding on a sledge, putting their beards together and throwing their arms about each other's neck. A happy fellow lies in the gutter fast asleep; another, just as tipsy, comes across the roadway, looks at his brother, draws his own wrapper round his limbs, and asking gods and men to pardon him, lies down tenderly in the puddle by his brother's side.

The social instincts are, in a Russian, of exceeding strength. He likes a crowd. The very hermits of his country are a social crew,—not men who rush away into lonely nooks, where, hidden from all eyes, they grub out caves in the rock and burrow under roots of trees; but brothers of some popular cloister, famous for its saints and pilgrims, where they drive a shaft under the convent wall, secrete themselves in a hole, and receive their food through a chink in sight of wondering visitors and advertising monks. Such were the founders of his church, the anchorets of Kief.

The first towns of Russia are Kief and Novgorod the Great; her capitals and holy places long before she built herself a kremlin on the Moskva, and a winter palace on the Neva. Kief and Novgorod are still her pious and poetic cities; one the tower of her religious faith, the other of her imperial power. From Vich Gorod at Kief springs the dome which celebrates her conversion to the Church of Christ; in the Kremlin of Novgorod stands the bronze group which typifies her empire of a thousand years.

CHAPTER VIII.

Kief.

KIEF, the oldest of Russian sees, is not in Russia Proper, and many historians treat it as a Polish town. The people are Ruthenians, and for hundreds of years the city belonged to the Polish crown. The plain in front of it is the Ukraine Steppe; the land of hetman and zaporogue; of stirring legends and riotous song. The manners are Polish and the people Poles. Yet here lies the cradle of that church which has shaped into its own likeness every quality of Russian political and domestic life.

The city consists of three parts, of three several towns—Podol, Vich Gorod, Pechersk; a business town, an imperial town, and a sacred town. All these quarters are crowded with offices, shops, and convents; yet Podol is the merchant quarter, Vich Gorod the government quarter, and Pechersk the pilgrim quarter. These towns overhang the Dnieper, on a range of broken cliffs; contain about seventy thousand souls; and hold, in two several places of interment, all that was mortal of the Pagan duke who became her foremost saint.

Kief is a city of legends and events; the preaching of St. Andrew, the piety of St. Olga, the conversion of St. Vladimir; the Mongolian assault, the Polish conquest, the recovery by Peter the Great.

The provinces round Kief resemble it, and rival it, in historic fame. Country of Mazeppa and Gonta, the Ukraine teems with story; tales of the raid, the flight, the night attack, the violated town. Every village has its legend, every town its epic, of love and war. The land is aglow with personal life. Yon chapel marks the spot where a grand duke was killed; this mound is the tomb of a Tartar horde; that field is the site of a battle with the Poles. The men are brighter and livelier, the houses are better built, and the fields are better trimmed, than in the North and East. The music is quicker, the brandy is stronger, the love is warmer, the hatred is keener, than you find elsewhere. These provinces are Gogol's country, and the scenery is that of his most popular tales.

Like all the southern cities, Kief fell into the power of Batu Khan, the Mongol chief, and groaned for ages under the yoke of Asiatic begs. These begs were idol-worshippers, and under their savage and idolatrous rule the children of Vladimir had to pass through heavy trials; but Kief can boast that in the worst of times she kept in her humble churches and her underground caves the sacred embers of her faith alive.

Below the tops of two high hills, three miles from that Vich Gorod in which Vladimir built his harem, and raised the statue of his pagan god, some Christian hermits, Anton, Feodosie, and their fellows, dug for themselves in the loose red rock a series of corridors and caves, in which they lived and died, examples of lowly virtue and the Christian life.

The Russian word for cave is "pechera," and the site of these caves was called Pechersk. Above the cells in which these hermits dwelt, two convents gradually arose, and took the names of Anton and Feodosie, now become the patron saints of Kief, and the reputed fathers of all men living in Russia a monastic life.

A green dip between the old town, now trimmed and planted, parts the first convent—that of Anton—from the city; a second dip divides the convent of Feodosie from that of his fellow-saint. These convents, nobly planned and strongly built, take rank among the finest piles in Eastern Europe. Domes and pinnacles of gold surmount each edifice; and every wall is pictured with legends from the lives of saints. The ground is holy. More than a hundred hermits lie in the catacombs, and crowds of holy men lie mouldering in every niche of the solid wall. Mouldering! I crave their pardons. Holy men never rust and rot. For purity of the flesh in death is evidence of purity of the flesh in life; and saints are just as incorruptible of body as of soul. In Anton's convent you are shown the skull of St. Vladimir; that is to say, a velvet pall in which his skull is said to be wrapped and swathed. You are told that the flesh is pure, the skin uncracked, the odour sweet. A line of dead bodies fills the underground passages and lanes—each body in a niche of the rock; and all these martyrs of the faith are said to be, like Vladimir, also fresh and sweet.

A stranger cannot say whether this tale of the

incorruptibility of early saints and monks is true or not; since nothing can be seen of the outward eye except a coffin, a velvet pall, and an inscription newly painted in the Slavonic tongue. A great deal turns on the amount of faith in which you seek for proof. For monks are men, and a critic can hardly press them with his doubts. Suppose you try to persuade your guides to lift the pall from St. Anton's face. Your own opinion is that even though human frames might resist the dissolving action of an atmosphere like that of Sicily and Egypt, nothing less than a miracle could have preserved intact the bodies of saints who died a thousand years ago in a cold, damp climate like that of Kief. You wish to put your science to the test of fact. You wish in vain. The monk will answer for the miracle, but no one answers for the monk.

Fifty thousand pilgrims, chiefly Ruthenians from the populous provinces of Podolia, Kief, and Volhynia, come in summer to these shrines.

When Kief recovered her freedom from the Tartar begs, she found herself by the chance of war a city of Polonia, not of Moscovy—a member of the Western, not of the Eastern, section of her race. Kief had never been Russ, as Moscow was Russ; a rude, barbaric town, with crowds of traders and rustics, ruled by a tartarized court; and now that her lot was cast with the more liberal and enlightened West, she grew into a yet more Oriental Prague. For many reigns she lay open to the arts of Germany and France; and when she returned to Russia, in the times of Peter the Great, she was not alone the noblest jewel in his crown, but a point of union, nowhere else to be found, for all the Slavonic nations in the world.

As an inland city Kief has the finest site in Russia. Standing on a range of bluffs, she overlooks a splendid length of steppe, a broad and navigable stream. She is the port and capital of the Ukraine; and the Malo-Russians, whether settled on the Don, the Ural, or the Dniester, look to her for orders of the day. She touches Poland with her right hand, Russia with her left; she flanks Galicia and Moldavia, and keeps her front towards the Bulgarians, the Montenegrins, and the Serbs. In her races and religion she is much in little; an epitome of all the Slavonic tribes. One-third of her population is Muscovite, one-third Russine, and one-third Polack; while in faith she is Orthodox, Roman Catholic, and United Greek. If any city in Europe offers itself to Panslavonic dreamers as their natural capital, it is Kief.

CHAPTER IX.

Panslavonia.

UNTIL a year ago, these Panslavonic dreamers were a party in the State; and even now they have powerful friends at Court. Their cry is Panslavonia for the Slavonians. Two years ago the members of this party called a congress in Moscow, to which they invited—first, their fellow-countrymen, from the White Sea to the Black, from the Vistula to the Amour; and next, the representatives of their race who dwell under foreign sceptres,—the Czeck from Prague, the Pole from Cracow, the Bulgar from Shumla, the Montenegrin from Cettigne, the Serb from Belgrade; but this gathering of the clans in Moscow opened the eyes of moderate men to the dangerous nature of this Panslavonic dream. A deep distrust of Russian life, as now existing, lies at the root of it; the dreamers hoping to fall back upon forms inspired by what they call a nobler national spirit. They read the chronicles of their race, they collect popular songs, they print peasant tales: and in these Ossianic legends of the Steppe, they find the germ of a policy which they call a natural product of their soil.

Like the Old Believers, these Panslavonians deny the Emperor and own the Tsar. To them Peter the Great is Antichrist, and the success of his reforms a temporary triumph of the Evil Spirit. He left his country, they allege, in order to study in foreign lands, the arts by which it could be overthrown. On his return to Russia no one recognised him as their prince. He came with a shaven face, a pipe in his mouth, a jug of beer in his hand. A single stroke of his pen threw down an edifice which his people had been rearing for a thousand years. He carried his government beyond the Russian soil; and, in a strange swamp, by the shores of a Swedish gulf, he built a palace for his court, a market for his purveyors, a fortress for his troops. This city he stamped with a foreign genius and baptized with a foreign name.

For these good reasons, the Panslavonians set their teeth against all that Peter did, against nearly all that his followers on the throne have done. They wish to put these alien things away, to resume their capital, to grow their beards, to wear their fur caps, to draw on their long boots, without being mocked as savages, and coerced like serfs. They deny that civilisation consists in a razor and a felt hat. Finding much to complain of in the judicial sharpness of German rule, they leapt to the conclusion that everything brought from beyond the Vistula is bad for Russia and the Russ. In the list of things to be kept out of their country, they include German philosophy, French morals, and English cotton prints.

A thorough Panslavonian is a man to make one smile; with him it is enough that a thing is Russian in order to be sworn the best of its kind. Now, many things in Russia are good enough for proud people to be proud of. The church-bells are musical, the furs warm and handsome, the horses swift, the hounds above all praise. The dinners are well served; the sterlet is good to eat; but the wines are not first-rate and the native knives and forks are bad. Yet patriots in Kief and Moscow tell you, with gravest face, that the vintage of the Don is finer than that of the Garonne, that the cutlery of Tula is superior to that of Sheffield. Yet these dreamers say and unsay in a breath, as seems for the moment best; for while they crack up their country right and wrong, in the face of strangers; they abuse it right and wrong when speaking of it among themselves. "We are sick, we are sick to death," was a saying in the streets, a cry in the public journals, long before Nicolas transferred the ailment of his country to that of his enemy the Turk. "We have never done a thing," wrote Khomakof, the Panslavonic poet; "not even made a rat-trap."

A Panslavonian fears free trade. He wants cheap cotton shirts, he wants good knives and forks; but then he shudders at the sight of a cheap shirt and a good fork on hearing from his priest that Manchester and Sheffield are two heretical towns, in which the spinners who weave cloth, the grinders who polish steel, have never been taught by their pastors how to sign themselves with the true Greek cross. What shall it profit a man to have a cheap shirt and lose his soul? The Orthodox clergy, seizing the Panslavonic banner, wrote on its front their own exclusive motto:—"Russia and the Byzantine Church;" and this priestly motto made a Panslavistic unity impossible; since the Western branches of the race are not disciples of that Byzantine Church. At Moscow everything was done to keep down these dissensions; and the question of a future capital was put off, as one too dangerous for debate. Nine men in ten of every party urge the abandonment of St. Petersburg; but Moscow, standing in the heart of Russia, cannot yield her claims to Kief.

The partizans of Old Russia join hands with those of Young Russia in assailing these Panslavistic dreamers, who prate of saving their country from the vices and errors of Europe, and offer— these assailants say—no other plan than that of changing a German yoke for either a Byzantine or a Polish yoke.

The clever men who guide this party are well aware that the laws and ceremonies of the Lower Empire offer them no good models; but in returning to the Greeks, they expect to gain a firmer hold on the practices of their Church. For the rest they are willing to rest in the hands of God, in the Oriental hope of finding that all is well at last. If nothing else is gained, they will have saved their souls.

"Their souls!" laugh the Young Russians, trained in what are called the infidel schools of France; "these fellows who have no souls to be saved!" "Their souls!" frown the Old Believers, strong in their ancient customs and ancient faith; "these men whose souls are already damned!" With a pitiless logic, these opponents of the Panslavonic dreamers call on them to put their thoughts into simple words. What is the use of dreaming dreams? "How can you promote Slavonic nationality," ask the Young Russians, "by excluding the most liberal and enlightened of our brethren? How can you promote civilisation by excluding cotton prints?" The Old Believers ask, on the other side, "How can you extend the true faith, by going back to the Lower Empire, in which religion was lost? How can you, who are not the children of Christ, promote His kingdom on the earth? You regenerate Russia! you, who are not the inheritors of her ancient and holy faith!"

Reformers of every school and type are coming to see the force which lies in a Western idea—not yet, practically, known in Russia—that of individual right. They ask for every sort of freedom; the right to live, the right to think, the right to speak, the right to hold land, the right to travel, the right to buy and sell, *as personal rights*. "How," they demand from the Panslavonians, "can the Russian become a free man while his personality is absorbed in the commune, in the empire, and in the church?"

"An old Russian," replies the Panslavonian, "was a free man, and a modern Russian is a free man, but in a higher sense than is understood by a trading people like the English, an infidel people like the French. Inspired by his church, a Russian has obtained the gifts of resignation and of sacrifice. By an act of devotion, he has conveyed his individual rights to his native prince, even as a son might give up his rights to a father in whose love and care he had perfect trust. A right is not lost which has been openly lodged in the hands of a compassionate and benevolent Tsar. The Western nations have retained a liberty which they find a curse, while the Russians have been saved by obeying the Holy Spirit."

Imagine the mockery by which an argument so patriarchal has been met!

"No illusion, gentlemen," said the Emperor to his first deputation of Poles. So far as they are linked in fortune with their Eastern brethren, the Poles are invited to an equal place in a great empire, having its centre of gravity in Moscow, its port of communication in St. Petersburg, not to a Japanese kingdom of the Slavonic tribes, with a mysterious and secluded throne in Kief.

Yet the Poles and Ruthenians who people the western provinces and the southern steppe will not readily give up their dream; and their genius for affairs, their oratorical gifts, their love of war, all tend to make them enemies equally dangerous in the court and in the field. Plastic, clever, adroit, with the advantage of speaking the language of the country, these dreamers get into places of high trust; into the professor's chair, into the secretary's office, into the aide-de-camp's saddle; in which they carry on their plot in favour of some form of government other than that under which they live.

CHAPTER X.

Exile.

A WEEK before the last rising of the Poles took place, an officer of high rank in the Russian service came in the dead of night, and wrapt in a great fur cloak, to a friend of mine living in St. Petersburg, with whom he had little more than a passing acquaintance—

"I am going out," he said, "and I have come to ask a favour, and say good-bye."

"Going out!"

"Yes," said his visitor. "My commission is signed, my post is marked. Next week you will hear strange news."

"Good God!" cried my friend; "think better of it. You, an officer of state, attached to the Ministry of War!"

"I am a Pole, and my country calls me. You, a stranger, cannot feel with the passions burning in my heart. I know that by quitting the service, I disgrace my general; that the government will call me a deserter; that if we fail, I shall be deemed unworthy of a soldier's death. All this I know, yet go I must."

"But your wife—and married one year!"

"She will be safe. I have asked for three

months' leave. Our passes have been signed; in a week she will be lodged in Paris with our friends. You are English; that is the reason why I seek you. In the drojki at your door is a box; it is full of coin. I want to leave this box with you; to be given up only in case we fail; and then to a man who will come to you and make this sign. I need not tell you that the money is all my own; and that the charge of it will not compromise you, since it is sacred to charity, and not to be used for war."

"It is a part, I suppose," said my friend, "of your Siberian Fund?"

"It is," said the soldier; "you will accept my trust?"

The box was left; the soldier went his way. In less than a week the revolt broke out in many places; slight collisions took place, and the Poles, under various leaders, met with the success which always attends surprise. Three or four names, till then unknown, began to attract the public eye; but the name of my friend's midnight visitor was not amongst them. General . . . grew into sudden fame; his rapid march, his dashing onset, his daily victory, alarmed the Russian court, until a very strong corps was ordered to be massed against him. Then he was crushed; some said he was slain. One night, my friend was seated in his chamber, reading an account of this action in a journal, when his servant came into the room with a card, on which was printed:

The Countess R——.

The lady was below, and begged to see my friend that night. Her name was strange to him; but he went out into the passage, where he found a pale, slim lady of middle age, attired in the deepest black.

"I have come to you," she said at once, "on a work of charity. A young soldier crawled to my house from the field of battle, so slashed and shot that we expected him to die that night. He was a patriot; and his papers showed that he was the young General.... He lived through the night, but wandered in his mind. He spoke much of Marie; perhaps she is his wife. By daylight he was tracked, and carried from my house; but ere he was dragged away, he gave me this card, and with the look of a dying man implored me to place it in your hands."

"You have brought it yourself from Poland?"

"I am a sufferer too," she said; "no time could be lost; in three days I am here."

"You knew him in other days?"

"No; never. He was miserable, and I wished to help him. I have not learned his actual name."

Glancing at the card, my friend saw that it contained nothing but his own name and address written in English letters; as it might be:

George Herbert,
Sergie Street,
St. Petersburg.

He knew the hand-writing. "Gracious heavens!" he exclaimed, "was this card given to you by General . . . ?"

"It was."

In half-an-hour my friend was closeted with a man who might intervene with some small hope. The Minister of War was reached. Surprised and grieved at the news conveyed to him, the Minister said he would see what could be done. "General Mouravieff," he explained, "is stern, his power unlimited; and my poor adjutant was taken on the field. Deserter, rebel,—what can be urged in arrest of death?" In truth, he had no time to plead, for Mouravieff's next dispatch from Poland gave an account of General . . .'s execution *by the rope*. On my friend calling at the War Office to hear if anything could be done, he was told the story by a sign.

"Can you tell me," inquired the Minister, "under what name my second adjutant is in the field? He also is missing." The caller could not help a smile. "You are thinking," said the Minister, "that this Polish revolt was organized in my office? You are not far wrong."

Archangel, Caucasus, Siberia—every frontier of the empire had her batch of hapless prisoners to receive. The present reign has seen the system of sending men to the frontiers much relaxed; and the public works of Archangel occupied for a time the place once held in the public mind by the Siberian mines. Not that the Asiatic waste has been abandoned as an Imperial Cayenne. Many great criminals, and some unhappy politicians, are still sent over the Ural heights; but the system has been much relaxed of late, and the name of Siberia is no longer that word of fear which once appalled the imagination like a living death. It is no uncommon thing to meet bands of young fellows going up the Ural slopes from Mesen and Archangel in search of fortune; going over into Siberia as into a promised land!

Many of the terrors which served to shroud Siberia in a pall have been swept away by science. The country has been opened up. The tribes have become better known. Tomsk, a name at which the blood ran cold, is seen to be a pleasant town, lying in a green valley at the foot of a noble range of heights. It is not far from Perm, which may be regarded as a distant suburb of Kazan. The tracks have been laid down, and in a few months a railroad will be made from Perm to Tomsk.

The world, too, has begun to see that a penal settlement has, at best, a limited lease of life. A man will make his home anywhere, and when a place has become his home, it must have already ceased to be his jail. It is in the nature of every penal settlement to become unsafe in time; and a province of Siberia, peopled by Poles, would be a vast embarrassment to the empire, a second Poland in her rear. Even now, long heads are counting the years when the sons of political exiles will occupy all the leading posts in Asia. Will they not plant in that region the seeds of a Polish power, and of a Catholic Church? It is the opinion of liberal Russians that Siberia will one day serve their country as England is served by the United States.

The exiles sent to the frontiers are of many kinds; noble, ignoble; clerical, lay; political offenders, cut-throats, heretics, coiners, schismatics; prisoners of the court, prisoners of the law, and prisoners of the church. The exiles sent away by a minister of police, by the governor of a province, are not kept in jail, are not compelled to work. The police has charge of them in a certain sense; they are numbered, and registered in books; and they have to report themselves at head-quarters from time to time. Beyond these limits they are free. You meet them in society; and if you guess they are exiles, it is mainly on account of their keener intelligence and their greater reserve of words. They either live on their private means, or follow the professions to which they have been trained. Some teach music and languages, some practise medicine or law; still more become secretaries and clerks to the official Russ. A great many occupy offices in the village system. In one day's drive in a tarantass I saw a dozen hamlets, in which every man serving as a justice of the peace was a Pole.

Not less than three thousand of the insurgents taken with arms in their hands during the last rising at Warsaw, were sent on to Archangel. At first the number was so great that an insurrection of prisoners threatened the safety of the town. The governor had to call in troops from the surrounding country, and the War-Office had to fetch back all the Prussian and Austrian Poles whom, in the first hours of repression, they had hurried to the confines of the Frozen Sea.

They lived in a great yellow building, once used as the arsenal of Archangel, before the government works were carried to the south; and their lot, though hard enough, was not harder than that of the people amongst whom they lived. They were gently used by the officers, who felt a soldierly respect for their courage, and a committee of foreign residents was allowed to visit them in their rooms. The food allowed to them was plentiful and good, and many a poor sentinel standing with his musket. in their doorways must have envied them the abundance of bread and soup.

In squads and companies these prisoners have been brought back to their homes; some to their families, others to the provinces in which they had lived. Many have been freed without terms; some have been suffered to return to Poland on the sole condition of their not going to Warsaw. A hundred, perhaps, remain in the arsenal building, waiting for their turn to march. Their lot is hard, no doubt; but where is the country in which the lot of a political prisoner is not hard? Is it Virginia? is it Ireland? is it France?

These prisoners are closely watched, and the chances of escape are faint; not one adventurer getting off in a dozen years. A Pole of desperate spirit, who had been sent to Mesen as a place of greater security than the open city of Archangel, slipped his guard, crawled through the pine-woods to the sea, hid himself in the forest, until he found an opportunity of stealing a fisherman's boat, and then pushed boldly from the shore in his tiny craft, in the hope of being picked up by some English or Swedish ship on her outward voyage. Four days and nights he lived on the open sea; suffering from chill and damp, and torn by the pangs of hunger and thirst, until the paddle dropt from his hands. His strength being spent, he drifted with the tide on shore, only too glad to exchange his liberty for bread. When the officer sent to make inquiries drove into Mesen, he found the poor fellow lying half dead in the convict ward.

Beyond this confinement in a bleak and distant land, the Polish insurgents do not seem to be physically ill used. Their tasks are light, their pay is higher than that of the soldiers guarding them, and some of the better class are allowed to work in cities as messengers and clerks. At one time they were allowed to teach—one man dancing, a second drawing, a third languages; but this privilege has been taken from them on the ground that in the exercise of these arts they were received into families, and abused their trust.

It is no easy thing to mix these Polish malcontents with the general race, without producing those results which a jealous police regard as a "corruption" of youth.

Man for man, a Pole is better taught than a Russian. He has more ideas, more invention, more practical talent. Having more resources, he cannot be thrown into the midst of his fellows without taking the lead. He can put their wishes into words, and show them how to act. A prisoner, he becomes a clerk; an exile, he becomes an overseer, a teacher —in fact, a leader of men. Sent out into a distant province, he gradually but surely asserts his rank. An order from the police cannot rob him of his genius; and when the ban is taken from his name, he may remain as a citizen in the town which gives him a career, and perhaps supplies him with a wife. He may get a professor's chair; he may be made a judge; if he has been a soldier he may be put on the general's staff.

All this time, and through all these changes, he may hold on to his hope; continuing to be a Pole at heart, and cherishing the dream of independence which has proved his bane. The country that employs him in her service is not sure of him. In her hour of trial he may betray her to an enemy; he may use the power in which she clothes him to deal her a mortal blow. She cannot trust him. She fears his tact, his suppleness, his capacity for work. In fact, she can neither get on with him nor without him.

In the meantime, Poles who have passed through years of exile into a second freedom are coming to be known as a class apart, with qualities and virtues of their own—the growth of suffering and experience acting on a sensitive and poetic frame. These men are known as the Siberians. A Pole with whom I travel some days is one of these Siberians, and from his lips I hear another side of this strange story of Exile life.

CHAPTER XI.

The Siberians.

"HE is one of the Siberians," says my comrade of the road, after quoting some verses from a Polish poet.

"One of the Siberians?"

"Yes," replies the Pole. "In these countries you find a people of whom the world has scarcely heard; a new people, I might say; for, while in physique they are like the fighting men who followed Sobieski to the walls of Vienna, they are in mind akin to the patient and laborious monks who have built up the shrines of Solovetsk. Time has done his work upon them. A sad and sober folk, they go among us by the name of our Siberians."

"They are Poles by birth?"

"Yes, Poles by genius and by birth. They are our children who have passed through fire; our children whom we never hoped to see in the living world. Once they were called our Lost Ones. In Poland we have a tragic phrase much used by parting friends:—'We never meet again!' For many years that parting phrase was fate. An exile, sent beyond the Ural Mountains, never came back; he was said to have joined our Lost Ones; he became to us a memory like the dead. We could not hope to see his face again, except in dreams. To-day that line is but a song, a recollection of the past; a refrain sung by the waters of Babylon. In Vilna, in Kazan, in Kief, in a hundred cities widely parted from each other, you will find a colony of Poles, now happy in their homes, who have crossed and re-crossed those heights; men of high birth, and of higher culture than their birth; men who have ploughed through the snows of Tomsk; who have brought back into the West a pure and bruised, though not a broken spirit."

"Are these pardoned men reconciled to the Emperor?"

"They are reconciled to God. Do not mistake me. No one doubts that the reigning Emperor is a good and brave man; high enough to see his duty; strong enough to face it, even though his feet should have to stumble long and often on the rocks. But God is over all, and his Son died for all; Alexander is but an instrument in His hands. You think me mystical! Because my countrymen believe in the higher powers, they are described by Franks who believe in nothing, as dreamers and spiritualists. We dream our dreams, we see our signs, we practise our religion, we respect our clergy, we obey our God."

"I have heard the Poles described as women in prayer, as gods in battle!"

"Like the young men of my circle," he continues, after a pause, "I took a part in the rising of '48; a poor affair, without the merit of being either Polish or Slavonic. That rising was entirely French. While young in years I had travelled with a comrade in the west of Europe; living on the Rhine, and on the Seine, where we forgot the religion of our mothers and our country, and learned to think and to speak of Poland as of a northern France. We called ourselves republicans, and thought we were great philosophers; but the idol of our fancies was Napoleon the Great, under whose banner so many of our countrymen threw away their lives. We ceased to appear at church, and even denied ourselves to the Polish priest. We hated the Tsar, and we despised the Russians, with all our souls. Two years before the republic was proclaimed in the streets of Paris, we returned to Warsaw, in the hope of finding some field of service against the Tsar; but the powers had been too swift for us; and Cracow, the last free city of our country, was incorporated with the Kaisar's empire on the day when I was dropped from the tarantass at my father's door. France bade us trust in her, and in the secret meetings which we called among our youthful friends, we gave up the good old Polish psalms and signs for Parisian songs and passwords. In other days we sang 'The Babe in Bethlehem,' but now, inspired with a foreign hope, we rioted through the Marseillaise. We had become strangers in the land, and the hearts of our people were not with us. The women fell away, the clergy looked askance, but the unpopularity of our new devices only made us laugh. We said to ourselves, we could do without these priests and fools; men who were always slaves, and women who were always dupes. As to the crowd of grocers and bakers,—

we thought of them only with contempt. Who ever heard of a revolution made by chandlers? We were noble, and how could we accept their help? The year of illusion came at length. That France to which every Polish eye was strained, became a republic; and then a troop of revellers, strong enough to whirl through a polka, threw themselves on the Russian guns, and were instantly sabred and shot down. Ridden over in the street, I was carried into a house; and, when my wounds were dressed, was taken to the Castle-royal, with a hundred others like myself, to await our trial by Commission, and our sentence of degradation from nobility, exile to Siberia, and perpetual service in the mines. My friend was with me in the street, and shared my doom."

"Had you to go on foot?"

"Well,—no. For Nicolas, though stern in temper, was not a man to break the law. Himself a prince, he felt a proud respect for the rights of birth; and as a noble could not be reduced to march in the gangs like a pedlar and a serf, our papers were made out in such a way that our privileges were not to end until we reached Tobolsk. There the permanent Commission of Siberia sat; and there each man received his order for the mines. We rode in a light cart, to which three strong ponies were tied with ropes; and when the roads were hard, we made two hundred versts a-day. Our feet were chained, so that we could not take off our boots by night or day; but the people of the steppe over which we tore at our topmost speed, were good and kind to us, as they are to exiles; giving us bread, dried fish, and whisky, on the sly. They knew that we were Poles, and, as a rule, their popes are only too much inclined to abuse the Poles as enemies of God; but the Russians, even when they are savages, have a tenderness of heart. They know the difference between a political exile and a thief; for the government stamps the thief and murderer on the forehead and the two cheeks with a triple vor; a black and ghastly stamp which neither fire nor acid will remove; and, if they think a Pole very wicked in being a Catholic they feel for his sufferings as a man. Twice I tried to escape from the mines; and on both occasions, though I failed to get away, the kindness of the poor surprised me. They dared not openly assist my flight, but they were sometimes blind and deaf; and often, when in hunger and despair I ventured to crawl near a cabin in the night, I found a ration of bread and fish, and even a cup of quass, laid ready on the window-ledge."

"Who put them there? and why?"

"Poor peasants, to whom bread and fish are scarce; in order to relieve the wants of some poor devil like myself."

"Then you began to like the people?"

"Like them! To understand them, and to see they were my brothers; but my heart was hard with them for years. I was a man of science, as they call it; and I told myself that in giving food to the hungry they were only obeying the first rude instincts of a savage horde. At length a poor priest came in a cart to the mines. Before his coming I had heard of him—his name—his mission—and his perils; for Father Paul was a free agent in his travels; having chosen this service in the desert snows, instead of a stall in some cathedral town, from a belief that poor Catholic exiles had a higher claim on him than sleek and fashionable folk. I knew, from the report of others, that he made the round of Siberia, sledging from mine to mine, from mill to mill, in order to keep alive in these Catholic exiles some remembrance of their early faith; to say mass, to hear confessions, to marry and baptize, to sanctify the new-made grave. Yet I hardly gave to him a second thought. What could he do for me; a poor priest, dwelling by choice in a savage waste, with no high sympathies and no great friends? He was not likely to adore Napoleon, and he was certain to detest Mazzini's name. How could I talk with such a man? The night when he arrived was cold, his sledge was injured, and the wolves had been upon his track. Some natural pity for his age and danger drew me to his side in our wooden shed; and after he was thawed into life, he spoke to us, even before he tasted food, of that love of God which was his only strength. When he had supped on our coarse turnip soup and a little black bread, he lay down on a mattrass and fell asleep. For hours that night I sat and gazed into his face, his white hair falling on his pillow, and his two arms folded like a cross upon his breast. If ever man looked like an angel in his sleep, it was Father Paul. Of such men is the Church of Christ.

"Next day I sought him in his shed, for our inspector turned this visit into a holiday for his Catholic prisoners; and there he spoke to me of my country and of my mother, until my heart was softened, and the tears ran down my face. Pausing softly in his speech, he bent his eyes upon me, as my father might have looked, and pressing me tenderly by the hand, said: 'Come unto me all ye that labour and are heavy laden, and I will give you rest.' 'Blessed are they that mourn; for they shall be comforted. Blessed are the meek; for they shall inherit the earth.' I had read these words a hundred times, for I was fond of the New Testament as a book of democratic texts; but I had never felt their force until they fell from the lips of Father Paul. I saw they were addressed to me. My mother was about me in the air. I laid down my philosophy, and felt once more like a little child."

His voice is low and mellow, but the tones are firm, and touch my ear like strings in perfect tune. After a pause, I asked him how his change of feeling worked in his relations to the Russians.

"A Christian," he replies, "is not a slave of the flesh. His first consideration is for God; his second for the children of God, not as they chance to dwell on the Vistula, on the Alps, on the Frozen Sea, but in every land alike. He yields up the sword to those who will one day perish by the sword. His weapon is the spirit, and he hopes to subdue mankind by love."

"Then you would yield the sword to any one who is proud and prompt enough to seize it?"

"No; the sword is God's to give, not mine to yield; and for His purposes He gives it unto whom He will. It is a fearful gift, and no man can be happy in whose grasp it lies."

"Yet many would like to hold it?"

"That is so. The man who first sees fire will burn himself. Observe how differently one thinks of war when one comes to see that men are really the sons of God. All war means killing some one. Which one? Would you like to think that in a future world some awful coil of fate should draw you into slaying an angel?"

"No, assuredly."

"Yet men are angels in a lower stage! We see things as we feel them. Men are blind, until their eyes are opened by the love of God; and God is nearest to the bruised and broken heart. Hosts of Siberians have come back to Poland; but among these exiles there is hardly one who has returned as he went forth."

"They are older."

"They are wiser. Father Paul, and priests like Father Paul—for he is not alone in his devotion—have not toiled in vain. Perhaps I should say they have not lived in vain; for the service which they render to the proud and broken spirit of the exile, is not the word they utter, but the doctrine they live. The poets and critics who have passed through fire, are known by their chastened style. They have put away France and the French. They read more serious books; they speak in more sober phrase. In everything except their love of God and love of country you might think them tame. They preach but little, and they practise much; above all, they look to what is high and noble, if remote, and set their faces sternly against the wanton waste of blood. They know the Russians better, and they did not need the amnesty, and what has followed it, in order to feel the brotherhood of all the Slavonic tribes."

"You are a Panslavonist?"

"No! We want a wider policy and a nobler word. The Panslavonic party has built a wall round Kief, and they would build a wall round Russia. They have a Chinese love of walls. Just look at Moscow; one wall round the Kremlin, a second wall round China-town, a third wall round the city proper. What we need is the old war-cry of St. George,—the patron of our early dukes, our free cities, and our missionary church."

CHAPTER XII.

St. George.

St. George is a patron saint of all the Slavonic nations; whether Wend or Serb, Russine or Russ, Polack or Czeck; but he is worshipped with peculiar reverence by the elder Russ. His days are their chief festivals; the days on which it is good for them to buy and sell, to pledge and marry, to hire a house, to lease a field, to start an enterprise. Two days in the year are dedicated in his name; corresponding in their idiom and their climate to the first day of spring and the last day of autumn; days of gladness to all men and women who live by tending flocks and tilling fields. On the first of these days the sheds are opened, the cattle go forth to graze, the shepherd takes up his crook, the dairy-maid polishes her pots and pans. The second day is a kind of harvest home, the labour of the year being over, the harvest garnered, and the flocks penned up. But George is a city saint as well as a rustic saint. His image is the cognizance of their free cities, and of their old republics; and the figure of the knight in conflict with the Dragon has been borne in every period by their dukes, their grand dukes, and their Tsars. His badge occurs on a thousand crosses, amulets, and charms; dividing the affections of a pious and superstitious race with images of the Holy Trinity and the Mother of God. The knight in conflict with the Dragon was proudly borne on the shield of Moscow hundreds of years before the Black Eagle was added to the Russian flag. That eagle was introduced by Ivan the Third; a prince who began the work (completed by his grandson, Ivan the Fourth,) of crushing the great boyars and destroying the free cities. Ivan copied that emblem from the Byzantine flag; a symbol of his autocratic power, which many of his people read as a sign that Devil Worship was the new religion of his army and his court. They saw in this black and ravening bird the Evil Spirit, just as they saw in the white and innocent dove the Holy Ghost. To soothe their fears, St. George was quartered on the Black Eagle; not in his talons, but on his breast; and in this form, the Christian warrior figures on every Russian flag and Russian coin.

St. George was the patron of an agricultural and pacific race; a country that was pious, rich, and free; and what he was in ancient times he still remains in the national heart. As the patron of soldiers he is hardly less popular with princes than peasants. Peter the Great engraved the figure of St. George on his sword; the Empress Catharine founded an order in his name; and Nicolas built in his honour a magnificent marble hall. Yet the high place and typical shrine of St. George is Novgorod the Great.

For miles above and miles below the red kremlin walls at Novgorod, the Volkhoff banks are beautiful with gardens, country-houses, and monastic piles. These swards are bright with grass and dark with firs; the houses are of Swiss-like pattern; and the convents are a wonder of the land. St. Cyril, and St. Anton, lend their names to masses of picturesque building; but the glory of this river-side scenery is the splendid monastery of St. George.

Built by Jaroslav, a son of St. Vladimir, on a ridge of high ground, near the point where Lake Ilmen flows into the river Volkhoff, the convent of St. George stood close to an ancient town called Gorod Itski—City of Strength—literally Fenced Town. Of this fenced town, a church, with frescoes older than those of Giotto, still remains; a church on a bluff, with the quaint old name of Spas Nereditsa; literally Our Saviour Beyond Bounds. In these old names old tales lie half entombed. From this fenced town, the burghers, troubled by a fierce democracy, appear to have crossed the river and built for themselves a kremlin (that is to say, a stone enclosure,) two miles lower down the stream, on a second ridge of ground, separated from the first by an impassable swamp. This new city, called Novgorod (New Town), was to become a wonder of the earth; a trading republic, a rival of Florence and Augsburg, a mother of colonies, a station of the Hanseatic League.

The old church of our Saviour Beyond Bounds, and the still older convent of St. George on the opposite bank, were left in the open country; left to the neglects of time and to the ravages of those

Tartar begs. who swept these plains from Moscow to the gates of Pskof.

Neglect, if slow, was steady in her task of ruining that ancient church, now become a land-mark only; but a land-mark equally useful to the critic of church history and to the raftsman guiding his float across the lake. As we leave the porch, an old man, standing uncovered near the door, calls out, "You come to see the church—the poor old church—but no one gives a ruble to repair the poor old church! It is St. George's Day; yet no one here remembers the dear old church! Look up at the Mother of God; see how she is tumbling down; yet no man comes to save her! Give some rubles, Gospodin, to our Blessed Lady, Mother of God!" The old man sighs and sobs these words in a voice that seems to come from a breaking heart.

St. George was able to defend his cells and shrines; and in all the ravages committed by Tartar hordes, the rich convent near Lake Ilmen was never profaned by Moslem hoof. Cold critics assume that the belt of peat and bog lying south of Novgorod for a hundred miles was the true defence; but the poets of Novgorod assert, in many a song and tale, that they owed their safety from the infidel spoilers to no freak of nature and no arm of flesh. St. George defended his convent and his city by a standing miracle; and, in return for his protecting grace, the people of this province come to kneel and pray, as their fathers for a thousand years have knelt and prayed, before his holy shrine.

My visit to the convent of St. George is paid

(in company with Father Bogoslovski, Russian pope, and Mr. Michell, English diplomat) on the autumnal festival of the saint. Three or four thousand pilgrims, chiefly from the town and province of Novgorod, camp in a green meadow; their carts unyoked; their horses tethered to the ground; their camp-fires lighted here and there. Each pilgrim brings a present to St. George; a load of hay, a sack of flour, a pot of wax, a roll of linen, an embroidered flag. That poor old creature, who can hardly walk, has brought him a ball of thread; a widow's mite, as welcome as an offering in gold and silver. Booths are built for the sale of bread and fruit; tea is fizzing on fifty stalls; grapes, nuts, and apples, are sold on every side. The peasants are warmly and brightly clad; the men in sheep-skin vests, fur caps, and boots; the women in damask gowns and jackets, quilted and puckered, the edges fringed with silver lace. A fine day tempts the women and children to throw themselves on the green in groups. Monks move among the crowd; country folk stare at the finery; hawkers chaffer with the girls; and more than one transparent humbug makes a market of relics and pious ware. Every one is in holiday humour; and the general aspect of the field in front of the convent gates is that of a village fair, with just a dash of the revival camp.

The worshippers are a placid, kindly, and (for the moment) a sober folk, with quaint expressions and old-world manners. On the boat, we hear a rustic say to his neighbour, "If you are not a noble, take your bundle off that bench and let me sit down; if you are a noble, go into the best cabin, your proper place." The neighbour sets his bundle down, and the new-comer drops into his seat, saying, "See, there is room for all Christians; we are equal here, being all baptized." An English churl might have said he had "paid his fare." On board the same boat a man replies to the steward, who wishes to turn him out of the dining-room, "Am I not a Christian, and why should I go out?" On hiring a boat to cross the river, Father Bogoslovski says to the oarsman, "Take your sheepskin; you will get a cold." "No; thank you," answers the waterman, "we never take cold if God is with us." Another boatman tells us we are doing a "good work" in visiting the shrines. "Once," he says, "I was sick and died; but I prayed to my angel Lazarus to let me live again. He listened to my prayers, not for my own sake, but for that of my brother, who had just come back from Solovetsk. My soul came back, and we were very glad. Your angel can always fetch back your soul, unless it has gone too far." Here stands a group of men; a young fellow with a basket of red apples, two or three lads, and an old peasant, evidently a stranger to these parts. "Eat an apple with me, uncle," says the young fellow to his elder; for a rustic, who addresses a stranger of his own age as "brother," always speaks to elderly ones as "uncle." "Very nice apples," says the stranger, "where were they blessed?" "In St. Sophia's, yonder; try them." Apples are blessed in church on August 6th, the Feast of the

Transfiguration; the earliest day on which such garden fruit is certain to be ripe. It is an old popular custom, maintained by the church, in the simple interest of the public health.

The scene is lovely. From the belfry of St. George — a shaft to compare with the Porcelain tower — you command a world of encircling pines, through which flow, past your feet, the broad and idle waters of the Volkhoff; draining the ample lake, here shining on your right. Below you spreads the deep and difficult marsh; and on the crests of a second ridge of land springs up a forest of spires and battlements, rich in all radiant hues; red walls, white towers, green domes, and golden pinnacles; here the kremlin and cathedral, there the city gate and bridge; and yonder, across the stream, the trading town, the bazaar, and Yaroslav's tower; the long and picturesque line of Novgorod the Great.

A bell of singular sweetness soothes the senses like a spell. At one stall you drink tea; no stronger liquor being sold at the convent gate. At a second stall you buy candles; to be lighted and left on the shrines within. At a third you get consecrated bread; a present for your friends and domestics far away. This fine white bread, being stamped with the cross and blessed, is not to be bought with money; for how could the flesh of our Lord be sold for coin? It is exchanged. You give a man twenty kopeks; he gives you a loaf of bread. Gift for gift is not barter — you are told — but brotherly love. On trying the same thing at an apple-stall, the result appears to you much the same. You pay down so many kopeks; you take up so much fruit; the quantity strictly measured by the amount of coin laid down. You see no difference between the two? Then you are not an Oriental, not a pilgrim of St. George.

Some twelve or fifteen thousand men and women bring their offerings, in kind and money, every spring and autumn to the shrine of this famous saint.

CHAPTER XIII.

Novgorod the Great.

SITTING at my window, gazing into space,—in front of me that famous tower of Yaroslav, from which once pealed the Vechie bell; and, lying beyond this tower, the public square, the bridge, the kremlin walls, Sophia's golden domes, and that proud pedestal of the present reign, which tells of a Russia counting already her thousand years of political life,—I fall a dreaming of the past, until the sceneries and the people come and go in a procession; not of dead things, but of quick and passionate men, alive with the energies of past and coming times.

What were the shapes and meanings of that dream? A wide expanse of wood and waste; forests of fir and silver-birch; with tarns and lakes on which the wild fowl of the country feed their young; and by the shores of which the shepherds and herdsmen watch their scanty flocks. In the midst of this wood and water stands a low red wall of stone, engirding a mass of cabins, with here and there a bigger cabin, from the peak of which springs a cross. A river rolls beneath the wall, the waters of which come from a dark and sombre lake. The space within the wall is a kremlin, an enclosure, and in this kremlin dwell a band of traders and craftsmen; holding their own, with watchful eye and ready hand, like the lodgers in a Syrian khan, against wild and predatory tribes. The life of these men is hard and mean; the air is bleak, the soil unfruitful; and the marauders prowl for ever at their gates.

A mist of time rolls up and hides the red stone wall and shingles from my sight, and, when it clears away, a vast and shining city stands exposed to view, with miles of street and garden, and an outer wall, of sweep so vast that the eye can hardly take it in, with massive gates and towers to defend these gates, of enormous strength. The river is now alive with boats and rafts; the streets are thronged with people, and a hundred domes and steeples glitter in the sun. The red kremlin, not now used as a castle of defence, is covered with public buildings; one a cathedral of gigantic size and surpassing beauty; another, a palace with a garden, belted by a moat; the citadel in which the traders nestled together for their common safety, having now become the seat of temporal and spiritual power. Long trains of horses file through the city gates, bringing in the produce of a thousand hamlets, which the merchants store in their magazines for export and expose in their bazaars for sale. These merchants bring their wares from East and West, and send them in exchange to the farthest ports and cities of the earth. Their town is a Free Town, to which men from all nations come and go; a Republic in the wilderness; a station of the Hanseatic league, devoting itself to freedom, commerce, and the liberal arts. The life of a great country flows into their streets and squares; from which run out again the prosperous purple tides into the unknown regions of ice and storm. Forth from her gates march out the colonists of the north; the men of Kem and Holmogory; men who are going forth to plant on the shores of the Arctic Sea the free institutions under which they live at home. A prince, elected by the people, serving while they list, sits in the chair of state, like a Podesta in Italian towns; but the actual power is in the hands of the Vechie: a popular Council, summoned by the ringing of a bell,—the great city bell—which swings in Yaroslav's tower.

Now comes a change, which seems to be less a change in the outward show than in the inner spirit of the place. The merchant has become a boyar, the nobleman a prince. Pride of the eye, and lust of the heart, are stamped upon every face. The rich are very rich; the poor are very poor; and men in cloth of gold affront and trample on men in rags. The streets—so spacious and so busy!—are disturbed by faction fights; and the Vechie bell is swinging day and night, as though some Tartar horde were at the gates. The boyars have grown too rich for freedom, and the ancients of the city sell their consciences for gold and state. Deeming themselves the equals of kings, they give their city not only the name of Great, but the name of Lord. On public documents they ask—as if in mockery—Who can stand against God, and Novgorod the Great?

Again falls the mist of time; and as it rolls away, the city, still as vast, though not so busy as of yore, seems troubled in her splendour by a sudden fear. The bell which tolls her citizens to council seems wild with pain, and men are hurrying to and fro along her streets; none daring, as in olden days, to snatch down lance and sword, and counsel his fellows to go forth and fight. For an enemy is nigh their gates, whom they have much offended, without having virtue enough to resist his arms. Ivan the Fourth, returning from a disastrous raid on the Baltic sea-board, hears that in his absence from Moscow the citizens of Novgorod, hating his rule, have sent an embassy to the Prince of Sweden, praying him to take them under his protection; and in his fury the tyrant swears to destroy that city, and to sow the site with salt. An army of Tartars and Kozaks is at the gates; an army sullen from defeat and loss, and only to be rallied by an orgy of drink and blood. Pale with terror, the citizens run to and fro; the women shriek and swoon; and help for them is none, until Father Nicolas, an ancient man, with flowing beard and saintly face, stands forward in their midst. A wild creature; an Elisha the prophet, a John the Baptist; he stands up in their meeting, naked from head to feet. Such a man suits the times; and as he offers to go forth and save the city from ruin, they gladly let him try. Nicolas marches forth, in his nakedness, to denounce his prince in the midst of his ravenous hordes; and when he comes into the camp, he walks up boldly to the Tsar. Ivan, himself a fanatic, listens to this naked man with a patience which his guards and ministers observe with wonder. "Blood-sucker and unbeliever!" cries the hermit, "thou who art a devourer of Christian flesh,—listen to my words. If thou, or any of these thy servants, touch a hair of a child's head in yon city, —which God preserves for a great purpose—then, I swear, by the Angel whom God has given unto me to serve me, thou shalt surely die; die on the instant, by a flash from heaven!" As he speaks, the sky grows dark, a storm springs up, and rages through the tents. A pall comes down, and covers the earth. "Spare me, fearful saint!" shrieks the Tsar; "the city is forgiven; and let me, in remembrance of this day, have thy constant prayers." On these conditions Nicolas withdraws his curse; and Ivan, marching into the city with his captives and his treasures, lodges in the kremlin and the palace, and kneeling before the shrine of St. Sophia, makes himself gracious to the people for the hermit's sake.

Once more a mist comes down—a thin white veil, which passes like a pout from an infant's face. The city is the same in size, in splendour, in the fulness of her fearful life. The Tsar, who went away from her gates low and humble, has come back, like a wild beast thirsting for blood and prey. His army camps beyond the walls, and a whisper passes through the city that the place is to be razed, the women given up to the Tartars, while the men and boys are to be put without mercy to the sword. The city razed! No fancy can take in the fact; for

Novgorod is one of the largest cities in Europe, a republic older than Florence, a capital larger than London, a shrine more sacred than Kief. Her walls measure fifty miles, her houses contain eight hundred thousand souls. Yet Ivan has doomed her to the dust. Telling off ten thousand gunners of his guard, and thirty thousand Tartars from the steppe, he gives up the republic to their lust, bidding them sack and burn, and spare neither man nor maid. They rush upon the gates; they scale the wall; they seize the bridge, the kremlin, the cathedral; and they make themselves masters of the city quarter by quarter and street by street. No pen will paint the horrors of that sack. The wines are drunk, the people butchered, the houses fired. Day by day, and week after week, the club, the musket, and the torch, are in constant use. The streets run blood, the river is choked with bodies of the slain. When the work of slaughter stops, and the Tartars are recalled into their camp, the tale of murdered men, women, and children, is found to be greater than the population of Petersburg in the present day. The desolation is Oriental and complete.

The city bell—the bell of council and of prayer—is taken down from Yaroslav's tower and sent to Moscow, where it hangs beside the Holy Gate,—an exile from the city it roused to arms, and haply speaking to some burgher's ear and student's heart of a time when Russian cities were equal to those of Italy and England, and her people were as free as those of Germany and France!

CHAPTER XIV.

Serfage.

SERFAGE has but a vague resemblance to the system of villeinage once so common in the West; and Serfage was not villeinage under another name. Villeinage was Occidental, Serfage Oriental.

Villein, aldion, colonus, fiscal, homme de pooste, are words which, in various tongues of Western Europe, mark the man who belonged to a master, and was bound by law to serve him. Whether he lived in England, Italy, or France, the man was stamped with the same character, and laden with the same obligation. He was a hedger and ditcher —churl, clod, lout, and boor—heavy as the earth he tilled, and swinish as the herds he fed. He could not leave his lord; he could not quit his homestead and his field. In turn, his master could not drive him from the soil, though he might beat him, force him to work, throw him into prison, and sell his services when he sold the land. But here the likeness of serf to either villein, aldion, colonus, fiscal, or homme de pooste, ends sharply. No one thought the villein was an actual owner of the soil he tilled, and in no country was the emancipation of his class accompanied by a cession of the land.

Serfage sprang from a different root, and in a different time. The Great Settlement which is the glory of Alexander's reign, can only be understood by reference to the causes from which Serfage sprang.

Some of the facts which prove this difference between Western villeinage and Eastern serfage lie beyond dispute. Villeinage was introduced by foreign princes, Serfage by native tsars. Villeinage followed a disastrous war; Serfage followed liberation from a foreign yoke. Villeinage came with the dark ages and passed away with them. Serfage came with the spreading light, with the rising of independence, with the sentiment of national life. Villeinage was forgotten by the Rhine, the Severn, and the Seine before Serfage was established on the Moskva and the Don.

In short, Serfage is an historical phase.

In one of the book-rooms of the Academy of Sciences, in Vassile Ostrof, St. Petersburg, you turn over the leaves of an early copy—said to be the first—of "Nestor's Chronicle," in which are many fine drawings of scenes and figures, helping you to understand the text. This copy is known as the Radzivil codex. Nestor wrote his book in Kief, a hundred years before that city was sacked by Batu Khan; and the pictures in the Radzivil codex give you the early Russian in his dress, his garb, and his ways of life. Was he in that early time an Asiatic, dressed in a sheep-skin robe and a sheepskin cap? In no degree. The Russian boyar dressed like a German knight; the Russian mujik dressed like an English churl.

In Nestor's time the Russians were a free people, ruled in one place by elective chiefs, in another place by family chiefs. They were a trading and pacific race; in the western countries settled in towns; in the eastern countries living in tents and huts. Novgorod, Pskof, and Hlynof, were free cities, ruled by elected magistrates, on the pattern of Florence and Pisa, Hamburg and Lübeck. In those days there was neither serf nor need of serf. But this old Russia fell under the Mongol yoke. Broken in the great battle on the Kalka, the country writhed in febrile agony for a hundred and eighty years; during which time her fields were scorched, her cities sacked, her peasants driven from their homes into the forest and the steppe. She had not yet raised her head from this blow, when Timur Beg swept over her prostrate form; an Asiatic of higher reach and nobler type than Batu Khan; a scholar, an artist, a statesman; though he was still an Asiatic in faith and spirit. Timur brought with him into Russia the code of Mecca, the art of Samarcand, the song of Ispahan. His begs were dashing, his mirzas polished. In the khanates which he left behind him on the Volga and in the Crimea, there was a courtesy, a beauty, and a splendour, not to be found in the native duchies of Nijni, Moscow, Riazan, and Tver. The native dukes and boyars of these provinces held from the Crim Tartar, known to our poets as the Great Cham. They swore allegiance to him; they paid him annual tribute; they flattered him by adopting his clothes and arms. The humblest vassals of this Great Cham were the Moscovite dukes, who called themselves his slaves, and were his slaves. Standing before him in the streets, they held his reins, and fed his horses out of their Tartar caps. They copied his fashions and assumed his names. Their armies, raised by his consent, were dressed and mounted in the Tartar style. They fought for him against their country, crushing those free republics in the north which his cavalry could not reach.

This fawning of dukes and boyars on the Great Cham brought no good to the rustic; who might see his patch of rye trodden down, his homestead fired, and his village cross profaned by gangs of marauding horse. Even when a Tartar Khan set up his flag on some river bank, as at Kazan, in some mountain gorge, as at Bakchi Serai, he was still a nomad and a rider, with his natural seat in the saddle, and his natural home in the tent. A little provocation stirred his blood, and when his feet were in the stirrups, it was not easy for shepherds and villagers to turn his lance. A cloud of fire went with him; a trail of smoke and embers lay behind him. No man could be sure of reaping what he sowed; for an angry word, an insolent gesture of his duke, might bring that fiery whirlwind of the Tartar horse upon his crops. What could he do, except run away? When year by year this ruin fell upon him, he left his cabin and his field; working a little here, and begging a little there; but never striking root into the soil. Now he was a pilgrim, then a shepherd, oftener still a tramp. To pass more easily to and fro, he donned the Tartar dress; a sheep-skin robe and cap; the robe caught in at the waist by a belt, and made to turn, so that the wool could be worn outwardly by day and inwardly by night. In self-defence he picked up Tartar words, and passed where he could pass for one of the conquering race.

Why should he plough his land for other men to spoil? While he was watching his corn grow ripe, the Khan of Crim Tartary, stung by some insult from the duke, might spur out rapidly from his luxurious camp at Bakchi Serai, and, sweeping through the plains from Perekop to Moscow, waste his fields with fire.

Like causes produce like effects. Nomadic lords produce nomadic slaves. The Russian peasant became a vagabond, just as the Syrian fellah becomes a vagabond when from year to year his crops have been plundered by the Bedouin tribes.

When Ivan the Fourth, having learned from the Tartar Begs how to rule and fight, broke up the Khanates of Kazan and Astrachan, and ventured to defy the lord of Bakchi Serai, he found himself an independent prince at the head of a country, rich in soil, in capital, and in labour, but with fields deserted, villages destroyed, populations scattered, and public roads unsafe. The land was not unpeopled; but the peasants had lost their sense of home, and the mujiks wandered from town to town. Labour was dear in one place, worthless in another. Half the land, even in the richer provinces, lay waste; and every year some district was scourged by famine, and by the epidemics which follow in the wake of famine. How were the peasants to be "fixed" upon the land?

For seventy years this question troubled the court in the Kremlin, even more than that court was troubled by church controversy, Tartar raid, and family strife; although within this period of seventy years St. Philip was murdered, the Great Cham burnt a portion of Moscow, Dimitri the legitimate heir was killed, and Boris Godounof usurped the throne. Ivan the Fourth tried hard to induce his people to return upon their lands; by giving up many of the crown estates; by building villages at his own expense; by coaxing, thrashing, forcing his people into order. Even if this reformer never used the term serf (krepostnoi, a man "fixed" or "fastened"), he is not the less—for good and ill—the author of that Russian Serfage which is passing away before our eyes.

CHAPTER XV.

A Tartar Court.

IN that gorgeous chamber of the Kremlin known as the Treasury of Moscow, stands an armed and mounted figure, richly dight, and called a boyar of the times of Ivan the Fourth. Arms, dress, accoutrements, are those of a Mirza, a Tartar noble; and an inscription on the drawn Damascus blade informs the pious Russian that there is but One God and that Mohammed is the prophet of God! Yet the figure is really that of a boyar of the times of Ivan the Fourth.

No prince in the line of Russian rulers is so great a puzzle as this Ivan the Fourth. In spite of his many atrocious deeds, he is still regarded by many of his critics as an able reformer and a patriotic prince. Much, indeed, must be said in his favour by all fair writers. To him the Moscovites owe their deliverance from the Tartar yoke. For them he conquered the kingdom of Kazan, the empire of Siberia, the Khanate of Astrachan. On all their frontiers he subdued the Crescent to the Cross. With Swedes and Poles he waged an equal, sometimes a glorious war. He opened his country to foreign trade; he built ports on the Baltic, on the Caspian, on the Frozen seas. The glories of his reign were of many kinds. He brought printers from the Rhine, and published the Acts of the Apostles in his native tongue. He sent to Frankfort for skilful physicians, to London for artificers in wood and brass. Collecting shipwrights at his river town of Vologda, he caused them to build for him a fleet of rafts and boats, on which he could descend with his treasures to the sea. He called a parliament of his estates to consult on the public weal. He reduced the unwritten laws of his country to a code. He put down mendicancy in his empire; laid his reforming hand on the clergy; and published a uniform confession of faith.

Ivan was a savage; though he was a popular savage. Terrible he was; but terrible to the rich and great. In fact, he was a reforming Tartar khan. If he taxed the merchants, he built hamlets for peasants at his private cost. If he crushed the free cities, he settled thousands of poor on the public lands. If he destroyed the princes and boyars as a ruling caste, he put into their places the official *chins*. If he ruled by the club, he also tried to rule by the printing-press. If he sacked Novgorod and Pskof, he built a vast number of churches, villages, and shrines. A builder by policy as well as by nature, he found an empire of logs, which he hoped to bequeath to his son as an empire of stone. Forty stone churches, sixty stone monasteries, owe their foundation to his care. He raised the quaint edifice of St. Vassili, near the Kremlin wall, which he called after his father's patron saint. He is said to have built a hundred and fifty castles, and more than three hundred communes.

Wishing to settle and civilise his people, the reformer sought his models in those Tartar provinces which he had recently subdued. Kazan and Bakchi Serai were nobler cities than Vladimir and Moscow; while the poorest Mirza of the Great Cham's court was far more splendid in arms and dress than any boyar in Ivan's court.

Ivan began to tartarize his kingdom by dividing it into two parts—personal and provincial; the first of which he ruled in person; the second by deputies wielding the power of Tartar begs. He raised a regular army—then the only one in Europe —which he armed and mounted in the Tartar style. He raised a body-guard to whom he gave the Tartar tafia; a cap that no Christian in his duchy was allowed to wear. Like the Great Cham, he set apart rooms in his palace for a harem; shut up his wives and daughters from the public eye; and changed the new fashion of excluding women from his court into a binding rule. His dukes and boyars followed him, until every house had a harem, and the seclusion of females was as strict in Moscow as in Bokhara and Bagdad.

These customs kept their ground until the times of Peter the Great. The land was governed by provincial begs, called boyars and voyevods; the army was drilled and dressed like Turkish troops; and the women were kept in harems like the Sultan's odalisques. Breaking through the customs introduced by Ivan, Peter opened the imperial harem;

showed his wife in public; and invited ladies to appear at court. Yet something of this Turkish fashion may still be traced in Russian family life, especially in the country towns. As every great house had its harem—a women's quarter, into which no stranger was allowed to set his foot; so every great family had a separate cemetery for the female sex. A few of these old cemeteries still remain as convents; for example, the Novo-Devictchie, Maidens' Convent, in the suburbs of Moscow; and the Convent of the Ascension, in the kremlin, near the Holy Gate; the burial-place of all the Tsarinas, from the time of Ivan the Terrible down to that of Peter the Great.

By subtle tricks and surprises, Ivan set his dukes and boyars quarrelling with each other, and when they were hot with speech, he would get them to accuse each other, and so despoil them both. In time he procured the surrender to him of nearly all their historical rights and titles; when, like a Sultan, he forced them to receive his gifts and graces, under their hands, *as slaves*. He introduced the Oriental practice of sending men, under forms of honour, into distant parts; inventing the political Siberia. His dukes were reduced in power, his boyars plundered of their wealth. The princes were too numerous to be touched, for in Ivan's time, every third man in Moscow was a prince; and an English trader used to hire such a man to groom his horse or clean his boots. Not many of the ancient dukes survived this reign; but the Narichkins, the Dolgoroukis, the Golitsins, and four or five others escaped; and these historical families look with patronising airs on the imperial race. The Narichkins have married with Romanofs. One of this house was offered the title of Imperial Highness, and declined it, saying proudly to his sovereign, "No, Sir, I am Narichkin." In the same spirit, Peter Dolgorouki, when he heard that the Emperor had taken away his title of Prince, wrote to his majesty, "How can *you* pretend to degrade *me?* Can you rob me of my ancestors, who were Grand Dukes in Russia when yours were not yet Counts of Holstein Gottorp?"

Moscow was governed like a Tartar camp. Ivan's body-guards (opritchniki), roved about the streets in their Tartar caps, abusing the people of every grade, boyar and burgher, mujik and peasant, as though they had been men of a different race and faith; robbing houses, carrying off women, murdering men; so that a stranger who met a company of these fellows in the Chinese town or under the Kremlin wall, imagined that the city had been given up to the soldiery for spoil.

This effort to settle the country on Tartar principles turned the Church against the Tsar; and led to the retirement of Athanasius, the dismissal of German, and the murder of Philip. St. Philip was the martyr of Russia; slain for defending his country and his church against this tartarizing Tsar.

Walk into the great cathedral of the Ascension any hour of the day in any season of the year, and —on the right wing of the altar—you will find a crowd of men and women prostrate before one silver shrine. It is the tomb of St. Philip, martyr and saint. Every one comes to him, every one kisses his temples and his feet. The murder of this saint is one of those national offences which a thousand years of penitence will not cleanse away. The penitent prays in his name; fasts in his name; burns candles in his name; and groans in spirit before the tomb, as though he were seeing forgiveness for some personal crime.

The tale of Philip's conflict with Ivan—a conflict of the Christian church against the Tartar court—may be briefly told.

CHAPTER XVI.

St. Philip.

EARLY in the reign of Ivan the Fourth (1539), a pilgrim, poor in garb and purse, but of handsome presence, landed from a boat at the Convent of Solovetsk. He came to pray; but after resting in the island for a little while, he took the vows and became a monk. Under the name of Philip, he lived for nine or ten years in his lowly cell. The monks, his brethren, saw there was some mystery in his life; his taste, his learning, and his manner, all announcing him as one of those men who belong to the higher ranks. But the lowly brother held his peace. Nine years after his arrival, the Prior of his convent died, and he was called by common assent to the vacant chair.

There was, in truth, a mystery in this monk. Among the proudest people in Moscow lived, in those days, the family of Kolicheff; to whom a son, Fedor, was born; the heir to a vast estate no less than to a glorious name. A pious mother taught the child to be good, according to her lights; to read about saints, to say long prayers, to listen for church-bells, and run with ardour to the sacrifice of mass. But being of noble birth, and having to serve his prince, Fedor was trained to ride and fence, to hunt and shoot, as well as to manage his father's forests, fisheries, and farms. At twenty-six, he was introduced to Ivan, then a child of four; and as the young prince took a fancy for him, he was much at court, admired by all women, envied by many men. It seemed as though Fedor Kolicheff had only to stay at court in order to become a minister of state. But his heart was never in the life he led; the Kremlin was a nest of intrigue; the country round the city was troubled by a thousand crimes. Distressed by what he saw going on, the favourite pined for a religious life; and quitting the world in silence, giving up all he possessed, he wandered from Moscow in a pilgrim's garb. Trudging on foot, a staff in his hand, a wallet by his side, he found his way through the trackless forests of the north; now stopping in a peasant's hut, where he toiled on the land for his daily food; now dropping down the Dvina on a raft, and tugging for his passage at the oars. Crossing over to the Convent he became a monk, a priest, a Prior, without betraying the secret of his noble birth and his place at court.

On coming into power, he set his heart on bringing back the Convent to her ancient life. He wore the frock of Zosima, and set up an image over Savatie's tomb. Taking these Worthies as his guides, he introduced the rule of assiduous work; invented forms of labour; making wax and salt; improving the fisheries and farms; building stone chapels; and teaching some of the fathers how to write and paint. Much of what is best in the convent, in the way of chapel, shrine, and picture, dates from his reign as Prior. But Philip was called from his cell in the Frozen Sea to occupy a loftier and more perilous throne.

Ivan, liking the old friend of his youth, consulted him on state affairs, and called him to the Kremlin to give advice. On these occasions, Philip was startled at the change in Ivan; who, from being a paladin of the cross, had settled down in his middle age into a mixture of the gloomy monk and the savage Khan. The change came on him with the death of his wife and the conquest of Kazan; after which events in his life he married two women, dressed himself in Tartar clothes, and adopted Asiatic ways. Like a chief of the Golden horde, he went about the streets of Moscow, ordering this man to be beaten, that man to be killed. The square in front of the Holy Gate was red with blood; and every house in the city was filled with sighs and groans.

Driving from their altars two aged prelates who rebuked his crimes, Ivan (in 1566) selected the Prior of Solovetsk, as a man who would shed a light on his reign without disturbing him by personal reproof. Philip tried to escape this perilous post; but the Tsar insisted on his obedience; and with heavy heart he sailed from his asylum in the islands, conscious of going to meet his martyr's crown.

Ivan had judged the monk in haste. Philip was no courtier; not a man to say smooth things to princes; for under his monk's attire he carried a heart to feel, an eye to see, and a tongue to speak. In passing from Solovetsk to Moscow, he passed through Novgorod; a city disliked by Ivan on account of her wealth, her freedom, and her laws; when a crowd of burghers poured from the gates, fell on their knees before him, and implored him, as a pastor of the poor, to plead their cause before the Tsar, then threatening to ravage their district and destroy their town. On reaching Moscow, he spoke to Ivan as to a son; beseeching him to dismiss his guards, to put off his strange habits, to live a holy life, and to rule his people in the spirit of their ancient dukes.

Ivan waxed red and wroth; he wanted a priest to bless, and not to curse. The tyrant grew more violent in his moods; but the new Metropolite held out in patient and unyielding meekness for the ancient ways. Once, when Philip was performing mass, the Tsar and his guards, attired in their Tartar dress, came into his church, and took up their ranks, while Ivan himself strode up to the royal gates. As Philip went on with his service, taking no notice of the Prince, a boyar cried, "It is the Tsar!" "I do not recognise the Tsar," said Philip, "in such a dress." The Tartar cap, the Tartar whip, were seen in every public place. The Tartar guards were masters of the city, and the streets were everywhere filled with the tumult of their evil deeds. They felt no reverence for holy things, and hurt the popular mind by treating the sacred images with disdain. In a procession, the Metropolite noticed one of these courtiers insolently wearing his Tartar cap. "Who is that man," asked Philip of the Tsar, "that he should profane with his Tartar costume this holy day?" Doffing his cap, the courtier denied that he was covered, and even charged the Metropolite with saying what was false. As every man in trouble went to his Metropolite for counsel, the boyars accused him of inciting the people against their Prince. When Ivan married his fourth wife, a thing unlawful and unclean, the Metropolite refused to admit the marriage, and bade the Tsar absent himself from mass. Rushing from his palace into the Cathedral of the Annunciation, Ivan took his seat and scowled. Instead of pausing to bless him, Philip went on with the service, until one of the favourites strode up to the altar, looked him boldly in the face, and said, in a saucy voice, "The Tsar demands thy blessing, priest!" Paying no heed to the courtier, Philip turned round to Ivan on his throne. "Pious Tsar!" he sighed; "why art thou here? In this place we offer a bloodless sacrifice to God." Ivan threatened him, by gesture and by word. "I am a stranger and a pilgrim on earth," said Philip; "I am ready to suffer for the truth."

He was made to suffer much, and soon. Dragged from his altar, stripped of his robe, arrayed in rags, he was beaten with brooms, tossed into a sledge, driven through the streets, mocked and hooted by armed men, and thrown into a dungeon in one of the obscurest convents of the town. Poor people knelt as the sledge drove past them, every eye being wet with tears, and every throat being choked with sobs. Philip blessed them as he went, saying, "Do not grieve; it is the will of God; pray,

pray!" The more patiently he bore his cross, the more these people sobbed and cried. Locked in his jail and laden with chains, not only round his ankles but round his neck, he was left for seven days and nights without food and drink, in the hope that he would die. A courtier who came to see him was surprised to find him engaged in prayer. His friends and kinsmen were arrested, judged, and put to death, for no offence save that of sharing his name and blood. "Sorcerer! dost thou know this head?" was one laconic message sent to Philip from the Tsar. "Yea!" murmured the prisoner, sadly; "it is that of my nephew Ivan." Day and night a crowd of people gathered round his convent-door, until the Tsar, who feared a rising in his favour, caused him to be secretly removed to a stronger prison in the town of Tver.

One year after this removal of Philip from Moscow (1569), Ivan, setting out for Novgorod, and calling to mind the speech once made by Philip in favour of that city, sent a ruffian to kill him. "Give me thy blessing!" said the murderer, coming into his cell. "Do thy master's work," replied the holy man; and the deed was quickly done.

The martyred saint remained a few years in Tver—whence he was removed to Solovetsk, an incorruptible frame; and lay in that isle until 1660, in the reign of Alexie, father of Peter the Great, in the days of tribulation, when the country was tried by sickness, famine, and foreign wars, his body was brought to Moscow, as a solemn and penitential act, by which the ruler and his people hoped to appease the wrath of Heaven. The Tsar's penitent letter of recall was read aloud before his tomb in Solovetsk, as though the saint could see and hear. The body was found entire, as on the day of sepulture; a sweet smell, as of herbs and flowers, coming out from beneath the coffin-lid. A grand procession of monks and pilgrims marched with the saint from Archangel to Moscow, where Alexie met them in the Kremlin gate, and carried the sacred dust into the Cathedral, where it was laid, in the corner of glory, in a magnificent silver shrine.

On the day of his coronation, every Emperor of Russia has to kneel before his shrine and kiss his feet.

CHAPTER XVII.

Serfs.

BORIS GODOUNOF, general, kinsman, successor of Ivan the Fourth, reduced the principle of Serfage into legal form (1601). An able and patriotic man, Godounof, designed to colonise his bare river-banks and his empty steppe. He meant no harm to the rustic—on the contrary, he hoped to do him good; his project of "fixing" the rustic on his land was treated as a great reform; and after taking counsel with his boyars, he selected the festival of St. George, the patron of free cities and of the ancient Russians, for his announcement that every peasant in the empire should in future till and own for ever the lands which he then tilled and held.

Down to that time, the theory of land was that of an Asiatic horde. From the Gulf of Venice to the Bay of Bengal the tenure of land might vary with race and clime; yet in every country where the Tartars reigned, the original property in the soil was everywhere said to be lodged in sultan, shah, mogul, and khan. The Russians, having lost the usage of their better time, transferred the rights which they acquired from Tartar begs and khans to their victorious prince.

This prince divided the soil according to his will; in one place founding villages for peasants, in a second place settling lands on a deserving voyavod, in a third place buying off an enemy with gifts of forests, fisheries, and lands; exactly in the fashion of Batu Khan and Timur Beg. This system of giving away crown lands was carried so far that when Godounof came to the throne (in 1598), he found his duchies and khanates consisting of a great many estates without labourers, and a great many labourers without estates. The peasants were roving hordes; and Godounof meant to fix these restless classes, by assigning to every family a personal and hereditary interest in the soil. The evil to be cured was an Oriental evil; and he sought to cure it in the Oriental way. The khans had done the same; and Godounof only extended and defined their method, so as to bring a larger area of country under spade and plough.

There is reason to believe that this festival of St. George (in 1601) was hailed by peasant and boyar as a glorious day; that the decree which established Serfage in Russia was accepted as a great and popular reform. To understand it, we must lay aside all notion of Serfage in Moscow and Tambof being the same thing as villeinage in Surrey and the Isle of France.

Serfage was a great Act of Colonisation. Much of what was done by Godounof was politic, and even noble; for he gave up to his people millions of acres of the Crown estates. The soil was given to the peasant on easy terms. He was to live on his land, to plough his field, to build his house, to pay his rates, and to serve his country in time of war. The chief concession made by the peasant, in exchange for his plot of ground, was his vagabond life.

To see that the serf—the man "fixed" on the soil—observed the terms of settlement, the prince appointed boyars and voyevods in every province as overseers; a necessary, and yet a fatal step. The overseer, a strong man dealing with a weak one, had been trained under Tartar rule; and just as the Tsar succeeded to the Khan, the Boyar looked upon himself as a successor to the Beg. Abuses of the system soon crept in; most of all that Oriental use of the stick, which the boyar borrowed from the beg; but a serf had to endure this evil—not in his quality of serf, but in his quality of Russian. Every man struck the one below him. A Tsar boxed a boyar, a boyar beat a prince. A colonel kicked his captain, and a captain clubbed his men. This use of the stick is in every region of the East a sign of lordship; and a boyar who could flog a peasant for neglecting to till his field, to repair his cabin, and to pay his rates, would have been more than man if he had not learned to consider himself as that peasant's lord.

Yet the theory of their holding was, that the peasant held his land of the Crown; even as the boyar held his land of the Crown. A bargain was made between two consenting parties—peasant and noble—under the authority of law, for their mutual dealing with a certain estate—consisting (say) of land, lake, and forest, with the various rights attached to ownership—hunting, shooting, fishing, fowling, trespass, right of way, right of stoppage, right of dealing, and the like. It was a bargain binding the one above as much as it bound the one below. If a serf could not quit his homestead, neither could the lord eject him from it. If the serf was bound to serve his master, he was free to save and hold a property of his own. If local custom and lawless temper led a master to fine and flog the serf, that serf could find some comfort in the thought that the fields which he tilled belonged to himself and to his commune by a title never to be gainsaid. A peasant's rhyme, addressed to his lord, defines the series of his rights and liabilities:

> "My soul is God's,
> My land is mine,
> My head's the Tsar's,
> My back is thine!"

A likeness to the serf may be found in the East, not in the West. The closest copy of a serf is the ryot of Bengal.

Down to the reign of Peter the Great the system went on darkening in abuse. The overseer of serfs became the owner. In lonely districts who was to protect a serf? I have myself heard a rustic ordered to be flogged by his Elder, on the bare request of two gentlemen, who said he was drunk and could not drive. The two gentlemen were tipsy; but the Elder knew them, and he never thought of asking for their proofs. A clown accused by a gentleman must be in the wrong. "God is too high, the Tsar too distant," says the peasant's saw. In those hard times the inner spirit overcame the legal form; and serfs were beaten, starved, transported, sold; but always in defiance of the law.

Peter introduced some changes, which, in spite of his good intentions, made the evil worse. He stopped the sale of serfs, apart from the estate on which they lived; a long step forward; but he clogged the beneficial action of his edict by converting the old house-tax into a poll-tax, and levying the whole amount of tax upon the lord, to whom he gave the right of collecting his quota from the serfs. A master armed with such a power is likely to be either worse than a devil or better than a man. Peter took from the religious bodies the right, which they held in common with boyars and princes, of possessing serfs. The monks had proved themselves unfit for such a trust; and as they held their lands by a title higher than the law can give, it was hard for a convent serf to believe that any part of the fields he tilled was actually his own.

Catharine followed Peter in his war on Tartar dress, beards, manners, and traditions; but she also set her face, as Peter had done, on much that was native to the soil. She meant well by her people, and the Charter of Rights, which she granted to her nobles, laid the foundation in her country of a permanent, educated, middle class. She studied the question of converting the serf's occupancy into freehold. She confiscated the serfs attached to convents, placing them under a separate jurisdiction; and she published edicts tending to improve the position of the peasant towards his lord. But these imperial acts, intended to do him good, brought still worse evils on his head; for serfage, heretofore a local custom—found in one province, not in the adjoining province—found in Moscow and Voronej, not in Harkof and Kief—was now recognised, guarded and defined by general law. Catharine's yearning for an ideal order in her states induced her to "fix" the peasant of Lithuania and Little Russia on the soil, just as Godounof had "fixed" the peasant of Great Russia, giving him a homestead and a property for ever on the soil. Paul, her son, took one stride forward in limiting the right of the lord to three days' labour in the seven; an edict which, though never put in force, endeared Paul's memory to the commons, many of whom regard him as a martyr in their cause. Yet Paul is one of those princes who extended the serf-empire. Paul created a new order of serfs in the Appanage Peasants, serfs belonging to members of the imperial house, just as the Crown Peasants belonged to the Crown domain.

Alexander the First set an example of dealing with the question by establishing his class of Free Peasants; but the wars of his reign left him neither time nor means for conducting a social revolution more imposing and more perilous than a political revolution, and after a few years had passed his Free Peasants fell back into their former state. Nicolas was not inclined by nature to reform; the old, unchanging Tartar spirit was strong within him; and he rounded the serfage system by placing the Free Peasants, colonists, foresters, and miners, under a special administration of the State. Every rustic in the land who had no master of his own became a peasant of the Crown.

But, from the reign of Ivan (ending in 1598) to the reign of Nicolas (ending in 1855), every patriot who dared to speak his mind inveighed against the abuse of serfage—as a thing unknown to his country in her happier times. Every false pretender, every reckless rebel, who took up arms against his sovereign, wrote on his banner "Freedom to the Serf." Stenka Razin (c. 1670) proclaimed, from his camp near Astrakhan, four articles, of which the first and second ran—deposition of the reigning house and liberation of the serfs! Pugacheff, in a revolt more recent and more formidable than that of Razin (c. 1770), publicly abolished serfage in the empire, taking the peasants from their lords, and leaving them in full possession of their lands. Pestel and the conspirators of 1825 put the abolition of serfage in the front of their demands.

Catharine's wish to deal with the question was inspired by Pugacheff's Letters of Emancipation; and on the very eve of his triumph in St. Isaac's Square, the Emperor Nicolas named a Secret Committee to report on the social condition of his empire, chiefly with the serf in view. At the end of three years, Nicolas, warned by their reports, drew up a series of Acts (1828-9), by which he founded an order of honorary citizens (not members of a guild), and set the peasants free from their lords. These Acts were never printed, for as time wore on, and things kept quiet, the Emperor saw less need for change. The July days in Paris frightened him; and having already sent out orders for the masters to treat their serfs like Christian men; and to be content in exacting three days' work in seven, according to the wish of Paul, the sovereign thought he had done enough. His Act of Emancipation was not to see the light.

In his later years the question troubled the Emperor Nicolas day and night. In spite of his glittering array of troops, he felt that serfage left him weak, even as the great division of his people into Orthodox and Old Believers left him weak. How weak these maladies of his country made him he only learned in the closing hours of his eventful life; and then (it is said) he told his son what he had done and left undone, enjoining him to study and complete his work.

It was well for the serf that Nicolas made him wait. The project of emancipation, drawn up under the eyes of Nicolas, was not a Russian document in either form or spirit; but a German state paper, based on the misleading western notion that Serfage was but villeinage under a better name. The principle laid down by Nicolas was, that the serf should obtain his personal freedom, and the lord should take possession of his land!

CHAPTER XVIII.

Emancipation.

ON the day when Alexander the Second came to his crown (1855), both lord and serf expected from his hands some great and healing act. The peasants trusted him, the nobles feared him. A panic seized upon the landlords. "What," they cried, "do you expect? The country is disturbed; our property will be destroyed. Look at these louts whom you talk of rendering free! They can neither read nor write; they have no capital; they have no credit; they have no enterprise. When they are not praying, they are getting drunk. A change may do in the Polish provinces; in the heart of Russia, never!" The Government met this storm in the higher circles by pacific words and vigorous acts; the Emperor saying to every one whom his voice could reach that the peril lay in doing nothing, not in doing much. Slowly but surely his opinion made its way.

Addresses from the several provinces came in. Committees of advice were formed, and the Emperor sought to engage the most active and liberal spirits in his task. When the public mind was opened to new lights, a Grand Committee was named in St. Petersburg, consisting of the ministers of state, and a few members of the Imperial Council, over whom

His Majesty undertook to preside. A second body, called the Reporting Committee, was also named, under the presidency of Count Rostovtsef, one of the pardoned rebels of 1825. The Grand Committee studied the principles which ought to govern emancipation; the Reporting Committee studied and arranged the facts. A mighty heap of papers was collected; eighteen volumes of facts and figures were printed; and the net results were thrown into a Draft.

The Reporting Committee having done their work, two bodies of Delegates from the provinces, elected by the lords, were invited to meet in the capital and consider this Draft. These Provincial Delegates raised objections, which they sent in writing to the Committee; and the new articles drawn up by them were laid before the Emperor and the Grand Committee, in an amended Draft.

Up to this point the Draft was in the hands of nobles and landowners; who drew it up in their class-interests, and according to their class-ideas. If it recognised the serf's right to personal freedom, it denied him any rights in the soil. This principle of "Liberty without Land" was the battle-cry of all parties in the upper ranks; and many persons knew that such was the principle laid down in the late Emperor's secret and abortive act. How could a committee of landlords, trembling for their rents, do otherwise? "Emancipation, if we must," they sighed, "but emancipation without the land." The Provincial Delegates stoutly urged this principle; the Reporting Committee embodied it in their draft.

Supported by these two bodies, it came before the Grand Committee. England, France, and Germany were cited; and as the villeins in those countries had received no grants of lands, it was resolved that the emancipated serfs should have no grants of land. The Grand Committee passed the amended Draft.

Then, happily, the Man was found. Whatever these scribes could say, the Emperor knew that forty-eight millions of his people looked to him for justice; and that every man in those forty-eight millions felt that his right in the soil was just as good as that of the Emperor in his crown. He saw that freedom without the means of living would be to the peasant a fatal gift. Unwilling to see a popular revolution turned into the movement of a class, he would not consent to make men paupers by the Act which pretended to make them free. "Liberty and Land"—that was the Alexandrine principle; a golden precept which he held against the best and oldest councillors in his court.

The acts of his Committees left him one course, and only one. He could appeal to a higher court. Some members of the Grand Committee, knowing their master's mind, had voted against the Draft; and now the Emperor laid that Draft before the Full Council, on the ground that a measure of such importance should not be settled in a lower assembly by a divided vote. Again he met with selfish views. The Full Council consists of Princes, Counts, and Generals—old men mostly—who have little more to expect from the crown, and every reason to look after the estates they have acquired. They voted against the Emperor and the serfs.

When all seemed lost, however, the fight was won. Not until the Full Council had decided to adopt the Draft, could the Emperor be persuaded to use his power, and to save his country; but on the morrow of their vote, the Prince, in his quality of Autocrat, declared that the principle of "Liberty and Land" was the principle of his Emancipation Act.

On the third of March, 1861 (Feb. 19, O. S.), the Emancipation Act was signed.

The rustic population then consisted of twenty-two millions of common serfs, three millions of Appanage peasants, and twenty-three millions of Crown peasants. The first class were enfranchised by that act; and a separate law has since been passed in favour of these Crown peasants and Appanage peasants, who are now as free in fact as they formerly were in name.

A certain portion of land, varying in different provinces according to soil and climate, was affixed to every "soul;" and Government aid was promised to the peasants in buying their homesteads and allotments. The serfs were not slow to take this hint. Down to January 1, 1869, more than half the enfranchised male serfs have taken advantage of this promise; and the debt now owing from the people to the Crown (that is, to the bondholders) is an enormous sum.

The Alexandrine principle of "Liberty and Land" being made the governing rule of the Emancipation Act, all reasonable fear lest the rustic, in receiving his freedom, might at once go wandering, was taken into account. Nobody knew how far the serf had been broken of those nomadic habits which led to serfage. Every one felt some doubt as to whether he could live with liberty and law; and rules were framed to prevent the return to those social anarchies which had forced the crown to "settle" the country under Boris Godounof and Peter the Great. These restrictive rules were nine in number: (1) a peasant was not to quit his village unless he gave up, once and for ever, his share of the communal lands; (2) in case of the commune refusing to accept his portion, he was to yield his plot to the general landlord; (3) he must have met his liabilities, if any, to the Emperor's recruiting officers; (4) he must have paid up all arrears of local and imperial rates, and also paid in advance such taxes for the current year; (5) he must have satisfied all private claims, fulfilled all personal contracts, under the authority of his cantonal administration; (6) he must be free from legal judgment and pursuit; (7) he must provide for the maintenance of all such members of his family to be left in the commune, as from either youth or age might become a burden to his village; (8) he must make good any arrears of rent which may be due on his allotment to the lord; (9) he must produce either a resolution passed by some other commune, admitting him as a member, or a certificate, properly signed, that he has bought the freehold of a plot of land, equal to two allotments, not above ten miles distant from the commune named. These rules—which are provisional only—are found to tie a peasant with enduring strictness to his fields.

The question, whether the serf is so far cured of his Tartar habit, that he can live a settled life without being bound to his patch of ground, is still unasked. The answer to that question must come with time, province by province, and town by town. Nature is slow, and habit is a growth. Reform must wait on nature, and observe her laws.

As in all such grand reforms, the parties most affected by the change were much dissatisfied at first. The serf had got too much; the lords had kept too much. In many provinces the peasants refused to hear the imperial rescript read in church. They said the priest was keeping them in the dark; for ruled by the nobles, and playing a false part against the Emperor, he was holding back the real letters of liberation, and reading them papers forged by their lords. Fanatics and impostors took advantage of their discontent to excite sedition, and these fanatics and impostors met with some success in provinces occupied by the Poles and Malo-Russ.

Two of these risings were important. At the village of Bezdna, province of Kazan, one Anton Petrof announced himself as a prophet of God, and an ambassador from the Tsar. He told the peasants that they were now free men, and that their good Emperor had given them all the land. Four thousand rustics followed him about, and when General Count Apraxine, overtaking the mob and calling upon them to give up their leader, and disperse under pain of being instantly shot down, the poor fellows cried, "We shall not give him up; we are all for the Tsar." Apraxine gave the word to fire; a hundred men dropped down with bullets in their bodies — fifty-one dead, the others badly hurt. In horror of this butchery the people cried, "You are firing into Alexander Nicolaivitch himself!" Petrof was taken, tried by court-martial, and shot in the presence of his stupified friends, who could not understand that a soldier was doing his duty to the crown by firing into masses of unarmed men.

A more singular and serious rising of serfs took place in the rich province of Penza, where a strange personage proclaimed himself the Grand Duke Constantine, brother of Nicolas, once a captive. Affecting Radical opinions, the "Grand Duke" raised a red flag, collected bands of peasants, and alarmed the country far and near. A body of soldiers, sent against them by General Dreniakine, were received with clubs and stones, and forced to run away. Dreniakine marched against the rebels, and in a smart action he dispersed them through the steppe, after killing eight and seriously maiming twenty-six. The "Grand Duke" was suffered to get away. The country was much excited by the rising, and on Easter Sunday General Dreniakine telegraphed to St. Petersburg his duty to the minister, and asked for power to punish the revolters by martial law. The minister sent him orders to act according to his judgment; and he began to flog and shoot the villagers until order was restored within the limits of his command. The "Grand Duke" was denounced as one Egortsof, a Milk-Drinker; and Dreniakine soon afterwards spread a report that he was dead.

The agitation was not stilled until the Emperor himself appeared on the scene. On his way to Yalta he convoked a meeting of Elders, to whom he addressed a few wise and solacing words: "I have given you all the liberties defined by the statutes; I have given you no liberties save those defined by the statutes." It was the very first time these peasants had heard of their Emperor's will being limited by law.

CHAPTER XIX.

Freedom.

"WHAT were the first effects of emancipation in your province?" I ask a lady.

"Rather droll," replies the Princess B. "In the morning, the poor fellows could not believe their senses; in the afternoon, they got tipsy; next day, they wanted to be married."

"Doubt—drunkenness—matrimony! Yes, it was rather droll."

"You see a serf was not suffered to drink whisky and make love as he pleased. It was a wild outburst of liberty; and perhaps the two things brought their own punishments?"

"Not the marrying, surely?"

"Ha! who knows?"

The upper ranks are much divided in opinion as to the true results of emancipation. If the liberal circles of the Winter Palace look on things in the rosiest light, the two extreme parties which stand aside as chorus and critics — the Whites and Reds, Obstructives and Socialists—regard them from two opposite points of view, as in the last degree unsound, unsafe.

When a Russian takes upon himself the office of critic, he is always gloomy, Oriental, and prophetic. He turns his face to the darker side of things; he groans in spirit and picks up words of woe. If he has to deal as critic with the sins of his own time and country, he prepares his tongue to denounce and his soul to curse; and his self-examination, whether in respect to his private vices or his public failings, is conducted in a dark, reproachful, and inquisitorial spirit.

In one house you fall among the Whites; a charming set of men to meet in drawing-room or club; urbane, accomplished, profligate; owners who never saw their serfs, landlords who never lived on their estates; fine fellows—whether young or old—who spent their lives in roving from St. Petersburg to Paris, and were known by sight in every gaming-house, in every theatre, from the Neva to the Seine. These men will tell you, with an exquisite smile, that Russia has come to the dogs. "Free labour!" they exclaim with scorn, "the country is sinking under these free institutions year by year—sinking in morals, sinking in production, sinking in political strength. A peasant works less, drinks more than ever. While he was a serf, he could be flogged into industry, if not into sobriety. Now he is master, he will please himself; and his pleasure is to dawdle in the dram-shop and to slumber on the stove. Not only is he going down himself, but he is pulling every one else down in his wake. The burgher is worse off; the merchant finds nothing to buy and sell. Less land is under plough and spade; the quantity of corn, oats, barley, and maize produced, is less than in the good old times. Russia is poorer than she was, financially and physically. Famines have become more frequent; arson is increasing; while the crimes of burglary and murder are keeping pace with the strides of fire and famine. As rich and poor we are more divided than we were as lords and serfs. The rich used to care for the poor, and the poorer classes lived on the waste of rich men's boards. They had an influence on each other, and always for their mutual good. In this new scheme, we are strangers when we are not rivals, competitors when we are not foes. A rustic cares for neither lord nor priest. A landlord who desires to live on his estate must bow and smile, must bend and cringe, in order to keep his own. The rustics rob his farm, they net his lake, they beat his bailiff, they insult his wife. His time is wasted in complaining, now to the police, now to the magistrate, now again to the cantonal chief. All classes are at strife, and the seeds of revolution are broadly sown."

In a second house you fall among the Reds; a far more dashing and excited set; many of whom have also spent much time in passing from St. Petersburg to Paris, though not with the hope of becoming known to croupiers and ballet-girls; men with pallid brows and sparkling eyes, who make a science of their social whims, and treat the emancipating acts as so many paths to that republic of rustics which they desire to see. "These circulars, reports and edicts were necessary," they allege, "in order to open men's eyes to the tragic facts. Our miseries were hidden; our princes were so rich, our palaces so splendid, and our troops so numerous, that the world—and even we ourselves—believed the Imperial Government strong enough to march in any direction, to strike down every foe. The Tsar was so great that no one thought of his serfs; the sun was so brilliant that you could not see the motes. But now that reign of deceit is gone for ever, and our wretchedness is exposed to every eye. You say we are free, and prospering in our freedom; but the facts are otherwise; we are neither free nor prosperous. The Act of Emancipation was a snare. Men fancied they were going to be freed from their lords; but when the day of deliverance came they found themselves taken from a bad master and delivered to a worse. A man who was once a serf became a slave. He had belonged to a neighbour, often to a friend, and now he became a property of the crown. Branded with the Black Eagle, he was fastened to the soil by a stronger chain. A false civilisation seized him; held him in her embrace; and made him pass into the fire. What has that civilisation done for him? Starved him; stript him; ruined him. Go into our cities. Look at our burghers; watch how they lie and cheat; hear how they bear false witness; note how they buy with one yard, sell with another yard. Go into our communes. Mark the dull eye and the stupid face of the village lout, who lives alone, like a wild beast, far from his fellows; part of the forest, as a log of wood is part of the forest. Observe how he drinks and shuffles; how he says his prayers, and shirks his duty, and begets his kind, with hardly more thought in his head than a wolf and a bear. This state of things must be swept away. The poor man is the victim of all tyrants, all impostors; the minister cheats him of his freedom, and the landlord of his field; but the hour of revolution is drawing nigh; and people will greet that coming hour with their rallying cry—More Liberty and more Land!"

A stranger listening to every one, looking into everything, will see that on the fringe of actual fact there are appearances which might seem to justify, according to the point of view, these opposite and extreme opinions; yet on massing and balancing his observations of the country as a whole, a stranger must perceive that under emancipation the peasant is better dressed, better lodged, and better fed; that his wife is healthier, his children cleaner, his homestead tidier; that he and his belongings are improved by the gift which changed him from a chattel into a man.

A peasant spends much money, it is true, in drams; but he spends yet more in clothing for his wife. He builds his cabin of better wood, and in the eastern provinces, if not in all, you find improvements in the walls and roof. He paints the logs, and fills up cracks with plaster, where he formerly left them bare and stuffed with moss. He sends his boys to school, and goes himself more frequently to church. If he exports less corn and fur to other countries, it is because, being richer, he can now afford to eat white bread and wear a cat-skin cap.

The burgher class and the merchant class have

been equally benefited by the change. A good many peasants have become burghers, and a good many burghers merchants. All the domestic and useful trades have been quickened into life. More shoes are worn, more carts are wanted, more cabins are built. Hats, coats, and cloaks are in higher demand; the bakeries and breweries find more to do; the teacher gets more pupils, and the banker has more customers on his books.

This movement runs along the line; for in the wake of emancipation every other liberty and right is following fast. Five years ago (1864), the Emperor called into existence two local parliaments in every province; a District Assembly, and a Provincial Assembly; in which every class, from prince to peasant, was to have his voice. The district Assembly is elected by classes; nobles, clergy, merchants, husbandmen; each apart, and free; the Provincial Assembly consists of delegates from the several District Assemblies. The District Assembly settles all questions as to roads and bridges; the Provincial Assembly looks to building prisons, draining pools, damming rivers, and the like. The peasant interest is strong in the District Assembly, the landlord interest in the Provincial Assembly; and they are equally useful as schools of freedom, eloquence and public spirit. On these local boards, the cleverest men in every province are being trained for civic, and if need be, parliamentary life.

On every side, an observer notes with pleasure a tendency of the villagers to move upon the towns and enter into the higher activities of civic life.

This tendency is carrying them back beyond the Tartar times into the better days of Novgorod and Pskoff.

In his Commune, a peasant may hope to pass through the dreary existence led by his mule and ox; his thoughts given up to his cabbage-soup, his buckwheat porridge, his loaf of black bread, and his darling dram. If he acquires in his village some patriarchal virtues—love of home, respect for age, delight in tales and songs, and preference for oral over written law; he also learns, without knowing why, to think and feel like a Bedouin in his tent, and a Kirghiz on his steppe. A rustic is nearly always humming old tunes. Whether you see him felling his pine, unloading his team, or sitting at his door, he is nearly always singing the same old dirge of love or war. When he breaks into a brisker stave, it is always into a song of revenge and hate. Bandits are his heroes; and the staid young fellow who dares not whisper to his partner in a dance, will roar out such a riotous squall:

> "I'll toil in the fields no more !
> For what can I gain by the spade ?
> My hands are empty, my heart is sore ;
> A knife ! my friend's in the forest glade !"

Another youth may sing:

> "I'll rob the merchant at his stall,
> I'll slay the noble in his hall ;
> With girls and whisky I'll have my fling,
> And the world will honour me like a king."

One of the most popular of these robber songs has

a chorus running thus, addressed in menace to the noble and the rich,—

> "We have come to drink your wine,
> We have come to steal your gold,
> We have come to kiss your wives!
>   Ha! ha!"

This reckless sense of right and wrong is due to that serfage, under which the peasants groaned for two hundred and sixty years. Serfage made men indifferent to life and death. The crimes of serfage have scarcely any parallel, except among savage tribes; and the liberty which some of the freed peasants enjoyed the most was the liberty of revenge.

Ivan Gorski was living in Tamboff, in very close friendship with a family of seven persons, when he conceived a grudge against them on some unknown ground, obtained a gun, and asked his friends to let him practise firing in their yard. They let him put up his target, and blaze away till he became a very fair shot, and people got used to the noise of his gun. When these two points were gained, he took off every member of the house. He could not tell the reason of his crime.

Daria Sokolof was employed as nurse in a family, and when the child grew up went back to her village; parting from her master and mistress on the best of terms. Some years passed by. On going into the town to sell her fruit and herbs, and finding a bad market, she went to her old home and asked for a lodging for the night. Her master was ill, and her mistress put her to bed. At two in the morning she got up, seized an Italian iron, crept to her master's room, and beat his brains out; then to her mistress's room, and killed her also. Afterwards she went into the servant's room, and murdered her; into the boy's room, and murdered him. A pet dog lay on the lad's coverlit, and she smashed its skull. She took a little money, not much; went home, and slept till daylight. No one suspected her, for no living creature knew she had been to the house. Twelve months elapsed before a clue was found; but as no witness of the crime was left, she could only be condemned to a dozen years in the Siberian mines. Her case excited much remark, and persons are even now petitioning the Ministry of Justice to let her off!

It is only by living in a wider field, by acting for himself, by gaining a higher knowledge of men and things, that the peasant can escape from the bad traditions and morbid sentiments of his former life. It will be an immense advantage for the empire of villages to become, as other nations are, an empire of both villages and towns.

CHAPTER XX.

Tsek and Artel.

THE obstacles which lie in the way of a peasant wishing to become a townsman are very great. After he has freed himself from his obligations to the Commune and the Crown, and arrived at the gates of Moscow, with his papers in perfect order, how is a rustic to live in that great city? By getting work. That would be the only trouble of a French paysan or an English plough-boy. In Russia it is different. The towns are not open and unwalled, so that men may come and go as they list. They are strongholds; held, in each case, by an army; in the ranks of which every man has his appointed place.

No man—not of noble birth—can live the burgher life in Moscow, save by gaining a place in one of the recognised orders of society,—in a Tsek, a Guild, or a Chin.

A Tsek is an association of craftsmen and petty traders, such as the tailoring Tsek, the cooking Tsek, and the pedling Tsek; the members of which pay a small sum of money, elect their own Elders, and manage their own affairs. The Elder of a Tsek gives to each member a printed form, which must be countersigned by the police not less than once a-year. A Guild is a higher kind of Tsek, the members of which pay a tax to the State for the privilege of buying and selling, and for immunity from serving in the ranks. A Chin is a grade in the public service; parted somewhat sharply into fourteen stages —from that of a certified collegian up to that of an acting privy-councillor. A peasant might enter a guild if he could pay the tax; but the impost is heavy, even for the lowest guild; and a man who comes into Moscow in search of work, must seek a place in some cheap and humble Tsek. He need not follow the calling of his Tsek—a clerk may belong to a shoemakers' Tsek, and a gentleman's servant to a hawkers' Tsek. But in one or other of these societies a peasant must get his name inscribed and his papers signed, under penalty of being seized by the police, and hustled into the ranks.

Every year he must go in person to the Office of Addresses, a vast establishment on the Tverskoi Boulevard, where the name, residence, and occupation of every man and woman living in this great city, are entered on the public books. At this Office of Addresses he has to leave his regular papers, taking a receipt which serves him as a passport for a week; in the meanwhile the police examine his papers, verify the Elder's signature, and mark them afresh with an official stamp. Every time he changes his lodging, he must go in person to the Office of Addresses, and record the change. A tax of three or four shillings a-year is levied on his papers by the police, half of which money goes to the Crown and half to the provincial hospitals. In case of poverty and sickness, his inscription in a Tsek entitles a man to be received into a government hospital should there be room for him in any of the wards.

To lose his papers is a calamity for the rustic hardly less serious than to lose his leg. Without his papers, he is an outlaw at the mercy of every one who hates him. He must go back at once to his village; if he has been lucky enough to get his name on the books of a Tsek, he must find the Elder, prove his loss, procure fresh evidence of his identity, and get this evidence countersigned by the police. Yet when a rustic comes to Moscow nothing is more likely than that his passport will be stolen. In Chinatown there is a rag fair, called the Hustling Market, where cheap-jacks sell every sort of ware—old sheepskins, rusty locks and keys, felt boots (third wear), and span-new saints in brass and tin. This market is a hiring-place for servants; and lads who have no friends in Moscow flock to this market in search of work. A fellow walks up to the rustic with a town-bred air: "You want a place? Very well; let me see your passport." Taking his papers from his boot—a peasant always puts his purse and papers in his boot—he offers them gladly to the man, who dodges through the crowd in a moment, while the rustic is gaping at him with open mouth. A thief knows where he can sell these papers, just as he could sell a stolen watch.

Having got his name inscribed in a Tsek, his passport signed by his Elder and countersigned by the police, the peasant, now become a burgher, looks about him for an Artel, which, if he have money enough, he proceeds to join.

An Artel is an association of workmen following the same craft, and organized on certain lines, with the principles of which they are made familiar in their village life. An Artel is a Commune carried from the country into the town. The members of an Artel join together for their mutual benefit and insurance. They elect an Elder, and confide to him the management of their concerns. They agree to work in common at their craft, to have no private interests, to throw their earnings into a single fund, and after paying the very light cost of their association, to divide the sum total into equal shares. In practical effect, the Artel is a finer form of communism than the Commune itself. In the village Commune they only divide the land; in the city Artel they divide the produce.

The origin of Artels is involved in mist. Some writers of the Panslavonic school profess to find traces of such an association in the tenth century; but the only proof adduced is the existence of a rule making towns and villages responsible, in cases of murder, for the fines inflicted on a criminal—a rule which these writers would find in the Frankish, Saxon, and other codes. The safer view appears to be, that the Artel came from Asia. No one knows the origin of this term Artel—it seems to be a Tartar word, and it is nowhere found in use until the reign of those tartarized Grand Dukes of Moscow, Ivan the Third and Ivan the Fourth. In fact, the Artel seems to have been planted in Russia with the Commune and the Serf.

The first Artel of which we have any notice was

a gang of thieves, who roamed about the country taking what they liked with a rude hand—inviting themselves to weddings and merry-makings, where they not only ate and drank as they pleased, but carried away the wine, the victuals, and the plate. These freebooters elected a chief, whom they called their ataman. They were bound to stand by each other in weal and woe. No rogue could go where he pleased—no thief could plunder on his personal account. The spoil was thrown into a common heap, from which every member of the Artel got an equal share.

These bandit Artels must have been strong and prosperous, since the principle of their association passed with little or no change into ordinary city life and trade. The burghers kept the word Artel; they translated ataman into Elder; and, in every minor detail, they copied their original, rule by rule. These early Artels had very few articles of association; and the principal were—that the members formed one body, bound to stand by each other; that they were to be governed by a chief, elected by general suffrage; that every man was appointed to his post by the Artel; that a member could not refuse to do the thing required of him; that no one should be suffered to drink, swear, game, and quarrel; that every one should bear himself towards his comrade like a brother; that no present should be received, unless it were shared by each; that a member could not name a man to serve in his stead, except with the consent of all. In after times these simple rules were supplemented by provisions for restoring to the member's heirs the value of his rights in the common fund. In case of death, these additional rules provided that the subscriber's share should go to his son, if he had a son; if not, to his next of kin, as any other property would descend. So far the estate was held to be a joint concern as regards the question of use, and a series of personal properties as regards the actual ownership. All these city Artels took the motto of "Honesty and Truth."

An Artel, then, was, in its origin, no other than an association of craftsmen for their mutual support against the miseries of city life, just as the Commune was an association of labourers for their mutual support against the miseries of country life. Each sprang, in its turn, from a sense of the weakness of individual men in struggling with the hard necessities of time and place. One body sought protection in numbers and mutual help against occasional lack of employment; the other against occasional attacks from wolves and bears, and against the annual floods of rain and drifts of snow. An Artel was a republic like a Commune; with a right of meeting, a right of election, a right of fine and punishment. No one interfered with the members, save in a general way. They made their own rules, obeyed their own chiefs, and were in every sense a State within the State. Yet these societies lived and throve, because they proved, on trial, to be as beneficial to the upper as they were to the lower class; an Artel offering advantages to employers of labour like those offered by a Commune to the ministers of finance and war.

If an English banker wants a clerk, he must go into the open market and find a servant, whom he has to hire on the strength of his character as certified from his latest place. He takes him on trial, subject to the chance of his proving an honest man. If a Russian banker wants a clerk, he sends for the Elder of an Artel, looks at his list, and hires his servant from the society, in that society's name. He seeks no character, takes no guarantee. The Artel is responsible for the clerk, and the banker trusts him in perfect confidence to the full extent of the Artel fund. If the clerk should prove to be a rogue — a thing which sometimes happens — the banker calls in the Elder, certifies the fact, and gets his money paid back at once.

These things may happen, yet they are not common. Petty thieving is the vice of every Eastern race, and Russians of the lower class are not exceptions to the rule; yet, in the Artels, it is certain that this tendency to pick and steal is greatly curbed, if not wholly suppressed. "Honesty and Truth," from being a phrase on the tongue, may come at length to be a habit of the mind. A decent life is strenuously enjoined, and no member is allowed to drink and game; thus many of the vices which lead to theft are held in check by the public opinion of his circle; yet the temptation sometimes grows too strong, and a confidential clerk decamps with his employer's box. Another merit of these Artels then comes out.

A robbery has taken place in the bank, a clerk is missing, and the banker feels assured that the money and the man are gone together. Notice is sent to the police; but Moscow is a very big city; and Rebrof, clever as he may be in catching thieves, has no instant means of following a man who has just committed in a bank parlour his virgin crime. But the Elder knows his man, and the members, who will have to suffer for his fault, are well acquainted with his haunts. Setting their eyes and tongues at work, they follow him with the energy of a pack of wolves on a trail of blood, never slackening in their race until they hunt him down and yield him up to trial, judgment, and the mines.

Bankers like Baron Stieglitz of St. Petersburg, merchants like Mazourin and Alexief in Moscow, have Artels of their own, founded in the first instance for their own work-people. On entering an Artel, a man pays a considerable sum of money—the average is a thousand rubles, one hundred and fifty pounds—though he need not always pay the whole sum down at once. That payment is the good-will; what is called the buying in. He goes to work wherever the Artel may appoint him. He gets no separate wages; for the payment is made to the Elder for one and all. So far this is share and share alike. But, then, the old rule about receiving presents has been much relaxed of late; and a good servant often receives from his master more than he receives as his share from the general fund. This innovation, it is true, destroys the old character of the Artel as a society for the mutual assurance of strong and weak; but in the progress of free thought and action it is a revolution not to be withstood, and hardly to be gainsaid.

One day, when dining with a Swede, a banker in St. Petersburg, I was struck by the quick eyes and ready hands of my host's butler, and, on my dropping a word in his praise, my host broke out, "Ha, that fellow is a golden man; he is my butler, valet, clerk, cashier, and master of the household—all in one."

"Is he a peasant?"

"Yes; a peasant from the South. I get him for nothing—for the price of a common lout."

"He comes to you from an Artel?"

"Yes, he and some dozen more; he is worth the other twelve."

"You pay the same wage for each and all?"

"To the Artel, so; but, hist! We make up for extra care and service by a thumping New Year's gift."

"Then the Artel is beginning to fail of its original purpose—that of securing to the weak, the idle, and the stupid men, as high a wage as it gave to the strong, the enterprising, and the able men?"

"Can you suppose that clever and pushing fellows will work like horses, all for nothing, now that they are free? A serf might do so; he lived in terror of the stick; he had no notion of his rights; and he had worked for others all his life. An Artel is a useful thing, and no one (least of all a foreign banker) wishes to see the institution fail; but it must go with the times. If it cannot find the means of drawing the best men into it by paying them fairly for what they do, it will pass away."

An Artel is a vast convenience to the foreign masters, whatever it may be to the native men.

CHAPTER XXI.

Masters and Men.

NOT in one town, in one province only, but in every town, we find two nations living in presence of each other; just as we find them in Finland and Livonia; an upper race and a lower; a foreign race and a native; and in nearly all these towns and provinces, the foreign race are the masters, the native race their men.

On the open plains and in the forest lands, this division into masters and men is not so strongly marked as in the towns. Here and there we find a stranger in possession of the soil; but the rule is not so; and while the towns may be said to belong in a rough way to the German, the country, as a whole, is the property of the Russ. The people may be parted into these two classes; not in commercial things only, but in professional study and in official life. The trade, the art, the science, and the power of Russia have all been lodged by law in the stranger's hand; the Russ being made an underling, even when he was not made a serf; and it is only in our own time—since the close of the Crimean war—that the crown has come, as it were, to the help of nature in recovering Russia for the Russ.

The dynasty is foreign. The fact is too common to excite remark; the first and most liberal countries in the world, so far as they have kings at all, being governed by princes of alien blood. In London the dynasty is Hanoverian; in Berlin it is Swabian; in Paris it is Corsican; in Vienna it is Swiss; in Florence it is Savoyard; in Copenhagen it is Holstein; in Stockholm it is French; in Brussels it is Cobourg; at the Hague it is Rhenish; in Lisbon it is Kohary; in Athens it is Danish; in Rio it is Portuguese. No bad moral would be therefore drawn from the fact of a Gottorp reigning on the Neva and the Moskva, were it not a fact that the Russian peasant had some reason to regard his prince as being not less foreign in spirit than he was in blood. The two princes who are best known to him—Ivan the Terrible and Peter the Great—announced, in season and out of season, that they were not Russ. "Take care of the weight," said Ivan to an English artist, giving him some bars of gold to be worked into plate, "for the Russians are all thieves." The artist smiled. "Why are you laughing?" asked the Tsar. "I was thinking that when you called the Russians thieves, that your Majesty forgot that you were Russ yourself." "Phoo!" replied the Tsar, "I am a German, not a Russ." Peter was loud in his scorn of everything Moscovite. He spoke the German tongue; he wore the German garb. He shaved his beard, and trimmed his hair in the German style. He built a German city, which he made his capital and his home, and he called that city by a German name. He loved to smoke his German pipe, and to quicken his brain with German beer. To him the new empire which he meant to found was a German empire, with ports like Hamburg, cities like Frankfort and Berlin; and he thought little more of his faithful Russ than as a horde of savages whom it had become his duty to improve into the likeness of Dutch and German boors.

To the imperial mind, itself foreign, the stranger has always been a type of order, peace, and progress, while the native has been a type of waste disorder, and stagnation. Hence, favours without end have been heaped on Germans by the reigning house, while Russians have been left to feel the presence of their government chiefly in the tax-collector, and the serjeant of police. This difference has become a subject for proverbs and jokes. When the Emperor asked a man who had done him service how he would like to be remembered in return, he said: "If your Majesty will only make me a German, everything else will come in time."

Ministers, ambassadors, chamberlains, have almost all been German; and when a Russian has been employed in a great command, it has been rather in war than in the more delicate affairs of state. The German, as a rule, is better taught and trained than the Russian; knowing arts and sciences, to which the Russian is supposed to be a stranger, now and for ever, as if learning were a thing beyond his reach. Peter made a law by which certain arts and crafts were to remain for ever in German hands. A Russian could not be a druggist, lest he should poison his neighbour; nor a chimney-sweep, lest he should set his shed on fire.

Such laws have been repealed by edicts; yet many remain in force, in virtue of a wider power than that of minister and prince. No Russian would take his dose of salts, his camomile pill, from the hands of his brother Russ. He has no confidence in native skill and care. A Russ may be a good physician, being quick, alert, and sympathetic; yet no amount of training seems to fit him for the delicate office of mixing drugs. He likes to lash out; and cannot curb his fury to the minute accuracy of an eye-glass and a pair of scales. A few grains, more or less, in a potion are to him nothing at all. In Moscow, where the Panslavonic hope is strong, I heard of more than one case in which the desire to deal at a native shop had sent the patriot to an untimely grave.

"You cannot teach a Russian girl," said a lady, who was speaking to me about her servants. "That girl, now, is a good sort of creature in her way; she never tires of work, never utters a complaint; she goes to mass on Saints'-days and Sundays; and she would rather die of hunger than taste eggs and milk in Lent. But I cannot persuade her to wash a sheet, to sweep a room, and to rock a cradle, in my English way. If I show her how to do it, she says, with a pensive look, that her people do things thus and thus; and if I insist on having my own way, in my own house, she will submit to force, under a sort of protest, and will then run home to tell her parents and her pope, that her English lady is possessed by an evil spirit."

The strangers who hold so many offices of trust in the country, and who form its intellectual aristocracy, are not considered in Berlin as of pure Germanic stock. They come from the Baltic provinces; from Livonia and Lithuania; but they trace their houses, not to the Letts and Wends of those regions, but to the old Teutonic knights. There can be no mistake about their energy and power.

Long before the days of Peter the Great they had a footing in the land; under Peter they became its masters; and ever since his reign they have been striving to subdue and civilise the people as their ancestors in Ost and West Preussen civilised the ancient Letts and Finns.

No love is lost between these strangers and natives, masters and men. The two races have nothing in common; neither blood, nor speech, nor faith. They differ like West and East. A German cuts his hair short, and trims his beard and moustache. He wears a hat and shoes, and wraps his limbs in soft, warm cloth. He strips himself at night, and prefers to sleep in a bed to frying his body on a stove. He washes himself once a-day. He never drinks whisky, and he loves sour-kraut. A German believes in science, a Russian believes in fate. One looks for his guide to experience, while the other is turning to his invisible powers. If a German child falls sick, his father sends for a doctor: if a Russian child falls sick, his father kneels to his saint.

In the north country, where wolves abound, a foreigner brings in his lambs at night; but the native says, a lamb is either born to be devoured by wolves or not; and any attempt to cross his fate is flying in the face of Heaven. A German is a man of ideas and methods. He believes in details. From his wide experience of the world he knows that one man can make carts, while a second can write poems, and a third can drill troops. He loves to see things in order, and his business going on with the smoothness of a machine. He rises early, and goes to bed late. With a pipe in his mouth, a glass of beer at his side, a pair of spectacles on his nose, he can toil for sixteen hours a-day, nor fancy that the labour is beyond his strength. He seldom faints at his desk, and he never forgets the respect which may be due to his chief. In offices of trust he is the soul of probity and intelligence. It is a rare thing, even in Russia, for a German to be bought with money; and his own strict dealing makes him hard with the wretch whom he has reason to suspect of yielding to a bribe. In the higher reaches of character he is still more of a puzzle to his men. With all his love of order and routine, he is a dreamer, and an idealist; and on the moral side of his nature he is capable of a tenderness, a chivalry, an enthusiasm, of which the Russian finds no traces in himself.

A Russ, on the other side, is a man of facts and of illusions; but his facts are in the region of his ideas, while his illusions rest in the region of his habits. It has been said, in irony of course, that a

Russian never dreams,—except when he is wide awake!

Let us go into a Russian workshop, and a German workshop; two flax-mills, say, at one of the great river towns.

In the first we find the master and his men of one race; with habits of life and thought essentially the same. They dine at the same table, eat the same kind of food. They wear the same long hair and beards, and dress in the same caftan and boots; they play the same games of draughts and whist; they drink the same whisky and quass; they kneel at the same village shrine; they kiss the same cross; and they confess their sins to a common priest. If one gets tipsy on Sunday night, the other is likely to have a fellow feeling for his fault. If the master strikes the man, it is an affair between the two. The man either bears the blow with patience, or returns it with the nearest cudgel. Of this family quarrel, the magistrate never hears.

In the second we find a more perfect industrial order, and a master with a shaven chin. This master, though he may be kind and just, is foreign in custom, and severe in drill. To him his craft is first, and his workmen next. He insists on regular hours, on work that knows no pause. He keeps the men to their tasks; allows no Monday loss on account of Sunday drink, and sets his face against the singing of those brigand songs, in which the Russian delights to spend his time. If his men are absent, he stops their wages; not wishing them to make up by night for what they waste by day. In case of need, he hauls them up before the nearest judge.

The races stand apart. A hundred German colonies exist on Russian soil; old colonies, new colonies, farming colonies, religious colonies. Everything about these foreign villages is clean and bright. The roads are well kept, the cabins well built, the gardens well trimmed. The carts are better made, the teams are better groomed, the harvests are better housed than among the natives; yet no perceptible influence flows from the German colony into the Russian commune; and a hamlet lying a league from such a settlement as Strelna or Sarepta is not unlikely to be worse for the example of its smiling face.

The natives see their master in an odious light. They look on his clean face, as that of a girl, and express the utmost contempt for his pipe of tobacco, his pair of spectacles, and his pot of beer. Whisky, they say, is the drink for men. Worse than all else, they regard him as a heretic, to whom Heaven may have given (as Arabs say) the power of the stick, but who is not the less disowned by the Church and cast out from God.

CHAPTER XXII.

The Bible.

A LEARNED father of the Ancient rite made some remarks to me on the Bible in Russia, which live in my mind as parts of the picture of this great country.

I knew that our Bible Society have a branch in St. Petersburg, and that copies of the New Testament and the Psalms have been scattered, through their agency, from the White Sea to the Black; but, being well aware that the right to found that branch of our Society in Russia was originally urged by men of the world in London upon men of the same class in St. Petersburg, and that the ministers of Alexander the First gave their consent in a time of war, when they wanted English help in men and money against the French, I supposed that the purposes in view had been political, and that this heavenly seed was cast into ungrateful soil. I had no conception of the good which our Society has been doing in silence for so many years.

"The Scriptures which came to us from England," said this priest, "have been the mainstay, not of our religion only, but of our national life."

"Then they have been much read?"

"In thousands, in ten thousands of pious homes. The true Russian likes his Bible—yes, even better than his dram—for the Bible tells him of a world beyond his daily field of toil, a world of angels and of spirits, in which he believes with a nearer faith than he puts in the wood and water about his feet. In every second house of Great Russia—the true, old Russia, in which we speak the same language and have the same God—you will find a copy of the Bible, and men who have the promise in their hearts."

In my journey through the country I find this true, though not so much in the letter as in the spirit. Except in New England and in Scotland, no people in the world, so far as they can read at all, are greater Bible-readers than the Russians.

In thinking of Russia, we forget the time when she was free, even as she is now again growing free, and take scant heed of the fact that she possessed a popular version of Scripture, used in all her churches and chapels, long before such a treasure was obtained by England, Germany, and France.

"Love for the Bible and love for Russia," said the priest, "go with us hand in hand, as the Tsar in his palace, and the monk in his convent, know. A patriotic government gives us the Bible, a monastic government takes it away."

"What do you mean by a patriotic government and a monastic government when speaking of the Bible?"

"By a patriotic government, that of Alexander the First and Alexander the Second; by a monastic government, that of Nicolas. The first Alexander gave us the Bible; Nicolas took it away; the second Alexander gave it us again. The first Alexander was a prince of gentle ways and simple thoughts; a mystic, as men of worldly training call a man who lives with God. Like all true Russians he had a deep and quick perception of the presence of things unseen. In the midst of his earthly troubles—and they were great—he turned into himself. He was a Bible-reader. In the Holy Word he found that peace which the world could neither give nor take away, and what he found for himself he set his heart on sharing with his children everywhere. Consulting Prince Galitzin, then his Minister of Public Worship, he found that pious and noble man—Galitzin was a Russian—of his mind. They read the Book together, and, seeing that it was good for them, they sent for Stanislaus, Archbishop of Mohiloff, and asked him why people should not read the Bible, each man for himself, and in his native tongue? Up to that time our sacred books were printed only in Bulgaric; a Slavonic speech, which people used to understand; but which is now an unknown dialect, even to the popes who drone it every day from the altar steps. Two English doctors—the good Patterson and the good Pinkerton—brought us the New Testament, printed in the Russian tongue; and, by help of the Tsar and his council, scattered the copies into every province and every town, from the frontiers of Poland to those of China. I am an old man now; but my veins still throb with the fervour of that day when we first received, in our native speech, the word that was to bring us eternal life. The books were instantly bought up and read; friends lent them to each other; and family meetings were held, in which the

Promise was read aloud. The popes explained the text; the elders gave out chapter and verse. Even in parties which met to drink whisky and play cards, some neighbour would produce his Bible, when the company gave up their games to listen while an aged man read out the story of the Passion and the Cross. That story spoke to the Russian heart; for the Russ, when left alone, has something of the Galilean in his nature; a something soft and feminine, almost sacrificial; helping him to feel, with a force which he could never reach by reasoning, the patient beauty of his Redeemer's life and death."

"And what were the effects of this Bible-reading?"

"Who can tell! You plant the acorn, your descendants sit beneath the oak. One thing it did for us, which we could never have done without its help,—the Bible drove the Jesuits from our midst,—and if we had it now in every house it would drive away these monks."

The story of the battle of the Bible Society and the Order of Jesus may be read in Joly, and in other writers. When that Order was suppressed in Rome, and the Fathers were banished from every Catholic State in Europe, a remnant was received into Russia, by the insane Emperor Paul, who took them into his favour in the hope of vexing the Roman Court, and of making them useful agents in his Catholic provinces. Well they repaid him for the shelter given,—not only in the Polish cities, but in the privatest recesses of his home. Father Gruber is said to have been familiar with every secret of the palace under Paul. These exiles were a band of outlaws, living in defiance of their spiritual chief and of their temporal prince; but while they clung with unslackening grasp to the great traditions of their Society, they sought, by visible service to mankind, the means of overcoming the hostility of popes and kings. No honest writer will deny that they were useful to the Russians in a secular sense, whatever trouble they may have caused them in a religious sense. They brought into this country the light of science and the love of art then flourishing in the West; and the colleges which they opened for the education of youth, were far in advance of the native schools. They built their schools at Moscow, Riga, St. Petersburg, Odessa, on the banks of the Volga, on the shores of the Caspian Sea. They sought to be useful in a thousand ways; in the foreign colony, at the military station, in the city prison, at the Siberian mine. They went out as doctors and as teachers. They followed the army into Astrachan, and toiled among the Kozaks of the Don; but while they laboured to do good, they laboured in a foreign and offensive spirit. To the Russ people, they were strangers and enemies; subjects of a foreign prince, and members of a hostile church. Some ladies of the court went over to their rite; a youth of high family followed these court ladies; then the clergy took alarm and raised their voices against the strangers. What offended the Russians most of all was the assumption by these Jesuits of the name of missionaries, as though the people were a savage horde not yet reclaimed to God and His Holy Church. Unhappily for the Fathers this title was expressly forbidden to the Catholic clergy by Russian law, and this assumption was an act of disobedience which left them at the mercy of the Crown.

But while the Emperor Paul was kind to them, these acts were passed in silence, and Alexander seemed unlikely to withdraw his favour from his father's friends. The issue of a New Testament in the native speech brought on the conflict and ensured their fate.

Following the traditions of their Order, the Jesuits heard the proposal to print the Bible in the Russian tongue, so that every man should read it for himself, with fear, and armed themselves to oppose the scheme. They spoke, they wrote, they preached against it. Calling it an error, they showed how much it was disliked in Rome. They said it was an English invasion of the country; and they stirred up the popes to attack it; saying it would be the ruin, not only of the Roman clergy, but of the Greek.

Alexander's eyes were opened to the character of his guests. The Bible was a comfort to himself, and why should others be refused the blessing he had found? Who were these men, that they should prevent his people reading the Word of Life?

A dangerous question for the Tsar to ask; for Prince Galitzin was close at hand with his reply. The worst day's work the Jesuits had ever done was to disturb this prince's family by converting his nephew to the Roman Church. Galitzin called it seduction; and seduction from the national faith is a public crime. When, therefore, Alexander came to ask who these men were, Galitzin answered, that they were teachers of false doctrine; disturbers of the public peace; men who were banished by their sovereigns; a body disbanded by their Popes. And then, in spite of their good deeds, they were sent away—first from Moscow and Petersburg, afterwards from every city of the empire. Their expulsion was one of the most popular acts of a long and glorious reign.

The Jesuit writers lay the blame of their expulsion on the Bible Societies.

From other sources, I learn that the New Testament was free until Alexander's death; and that the copies found their way into every city and village of the land. With the death of Alexander the First came a change. After the conspiracy of 1825, the new Emperor listened to his Black clergy, and the Bible was placed under close arrest.

The Russian Bible Society was called a Russian Parliament. All parties in the state were represented on the board of management; Orthodox bishops sitting next to Old Believers, and Old Believers next to Dissenting priests. The Bible, in which they all believed, was a common ground, on which they could meet and exchange the words of peace. But Nicolas, ruling by the sword, had no desire to see these boards pursuing their active and independent course; and his monks had little trouble in persuading him to replace the Bible by an official Book of Saints.

CHAPTER XXIII.

Parish Priests.

In this Empire of Villages, there is a force of six hundred and ten thousand parish priests (a' little more or less); each parish priest the centre of a circle, who regard him, not only as a man of God, ordained to bless in His holy name, but as a father to advise them in weal and woe. These priests are not only popular, but in country villages they are themselves the people.

. Father Peter, the village pope, is a countryman like the members of his flock. In his youth, he must have been at school and college; a smart lad, perhaps, alert of tongue and learned in decrees and canons; but he has long since sobered down into the dull and patient priest you see. In speech, in gait, in dress, he is exactly like the peasants in yon dram-shop and yon field. His cabin is built of logs; his wife grows girkins, which she carries in a creel to the nearest town for sale; and the reverend gentleman puts his right hand on the plough. He does not preach and teach; for he has little to say, and not a word that any of his neighbours would care to hear. Knowing that his lot in life is fixed, he has no inducement to refresh his mind with learning, and to burnish up his oratorical arms. The world slips past him, unperceived; and with his grip on the peasant's spade, he sinks insensibly into the peasant's class. Yet Peter's life, though it may be hard and poor, is not without lines of natural grace; the more affecting from the homeliness of everything around. His cabin is very clean; some flower-pots stand on his window-sill; a heap of books loads his presses; and his walls are picturesque with prints of chapel and saint. A pale and comely wife is sitting near his door, knitting her children's hose, and watching the urchins at their play. Those boys are singing beneath a tree; singing with soft, sad faces one of their ritual psalms. A calm and tender influence flows from his house into the neighbouring sheds. The dullest hind in the hamlet sees that the pastor's little ones are kept in order, and that his cabin is the pattern of a tidy village hut.

The pastor has his patch of land to till, his bit of garden ground to tend; but on every side you find the homely folk about him helping in his labour, each peasant in his turn, so as to make his duties light. Presents of many kinds are made to him; ducklings, fish, cucumbers, even shoes and wraps, as well as angel-day offerings and benediction-fees. A priest is so great a man in a village, that even when he is a tipsy, idle fellow, he is treated by his parishioners with a child-like duty and respect. The pastor can do much to help his flock, not only in their spiritual wants, but in their secular affairs. In any quarrel with the police, it is of great importance to a peasant that his priest should take his part; and the pastor commonly takes his neighbour's part, not only because he himself is poor, and knows the man, but because he hates all public officers and suspects all men in power.

A great day for the parish priest is that on which a child is born in his Commune.

When Dimitri (the peasant living in yon big house is called Dimitri) hears that a son has been given to him, he runs for his priest, and Father Peter comes in stately haste to welcome and bless the little one. Finding the baby swinging in his liulka, Father Peter puts on his cope, unclasps his book, turns his face to the holy icons, and begins his prayer. "Lord God," he cries, "we beg Thee to send down the light of Thy face upon this child, Thy servant Constantine; and be he signed with the cross of Thy Only-begotten Son. Amen."

In two or three weeks the christening of little Constantine, "Servant of God," takes place. When the rite is performed at home, the house has to be turned, as it were, into a chapel for the nonce; no difficult thing, as parlour, kitchen, hall, saloon, are decorated with the Son, the Mother, and the patron saint. A room is set apart for the office; a rug is spread before the sacred pictures; and on a table are laid three candles, a fine napkin, and a glass of water from the well. A silver-gilt basin is sent from the village church. Attended by his reader and his deacon, each carrying a bundle, Father Peter walks to the house, bearing a cross and singing a psalm, while the censer is swung before him in the street.

The rite then given is long and solemn; the ceremony consisting of many parts. First comes the act of driving out the fiends; when the pope, not yet in his perfect robes, takes up the baby, breathes on his face, crosses him three times on temple, breast, and lips, and exorcises the devil and all his imps; ending with the words, "May every evil and unclean spirit that has taken up his abode in this infant's heart depart from hence!" Then comes the act of Renouncing the Evil One and all his works in the baby's name. "Dost thou renounce the devil?" asks the pope; on which the sponsors turn, with the child, towards the setting sun, that land of shadows in which the Prince of Darkness is supposed to dwell, and answer, each, "I have renounced him." "Spit on him!" cries the pope, who jets his own saliva into a corner, as though the devil were present in the room. The sponsors spit in turn. Here follows the Confession of Faith; the sponsors being asked whether they believe that Christ is King and God; and on answering that they believe in Him as King and God, are told to fall down and worship Him as such. Next comes the Rite of Baptism, when the pope puts on his brightest robe, the parents are sent away, and the child is left to his godfathers and godmothers. A taper is put into each sponsor's hand; the candles near the font are lighted; incense is flung about; the reader and deacon sing; and the pope inaudibly recites a prayer. The water is blessed by the pope dipping his right hand into it three times, by breathing on it, praying over it, and signing it with the cross. He uses for that purpose a feather which has been dipped into holy oil. The child is anointed five times; first on the forehead, with this phrase, "Constantine, the Servant of God, is anointed with the oil of gladness;" next on the chest, to heal his soul and body; then on the two ears, to quicken his sense of the Word; afterwards on his hands and feet, to do God's will and walk in his way. Seized by the pope, the child is now plunged into the font three times, by rapid dips; the priest repeating at each dip, "Constantine, the Servant of God, is now baptized in the name of the Father, and of the Son, and of the Holy Ghost." If the young Christian is not drowned in the font (as sometimes happens), he is clad in white, he receives his name, his guardian angel, and his cross.

The Rite of Baptism ended, the Sacrament of Unction opens. This sacrament, called the Seal of the Gift of the Holy Spirit, is said to represent the "laying on of hands" in the early Christian church. With a small feather, dipped once more into the sacred oil, the pope again touches the baby's forehead, chest, lips, hands, and feet, saying each time, "The Seal of the Gift of the Holy Spirit;" on which reader, deacon, and priest all break into chaunts of allelujah! After Unction, comes the Act of Sacrifice; when the child, who has nothing else of his own to give, offers up the *hair of his head*. Taking a pair of shears, the pope snips off the down in four places from the baby's head, making a cross, and saying, as he cuts each piece away, "Constantine, the Servant of God, is shorn in Thy name."

The hair is thrown into the font; more litany is sung; and the child is at length given back, fatigued and sleepy, into his mother's arms.

Ten or twelve days later, Constantine must be taken by his mother to mass, and receive the sacrament, as a sign of his visible acceptance in the Church. A nurse walks up the steps before the royal gates; and when the deacon comes forward with the cup in his hand, she goes to meet him. He takes a small spoon and puts a drop of wine into the infant's mouth, saying, "Constantine, the Servant of God, communicates in the name of the Father, Son, and Holy Ghost." Later in the service, the pope himself takes up the child, and pressing his nose against the icons on the screen, cries loudly, "Constantine, the Servant of God, is now received into the Church of Christ."

Not less grand a time for Father Peter is a wedding-day. The rite is longer and the fees are more. Old Tartar customs keep their hold on these common folk, if not on the higher ranks, and courtship, as we understand it, is a thing unknown. A match is made by the Proposeress and the parents, not by the youth and maiden—for in habit, if not in law, the sexes live apart, and do not see much of each other until the knot is tied.

A servant came into the parlour of a house in which I was staying as a guest—came in simpering and crying—to say that she wished to leave her place. "To leave! For what cause?"

Well, she was going to be married.

"Married, Maria!" cried her mistress; "when?"

"The day after next," replied the woman, shedding tears.

"So soon, Maria! And what sort of man are you going to wed?"

The woman dropped her eyes. She could not say; she had not seen him yet. The Proposeress had done it all, and sent her word to appear in church at four o'clock, the hour for marrying persons of her class.

"You really mean to take this man whom you have never seen?"

"I must," said the woman, "the prayers have been put up in church."

"Do the parish popes raise no objections to such marriages?"

"No," laughed the lady. "Why should they object? A wedding brings them fees; and in their cabins you will find more children than kopeks."

The livings held by the parish clergy are not rich. Some few city holdings may be worth three or four hundred pounds a-year; these are the prizes. Few of the country pastors have an income, over and above the kitchen-garden and plough of land, exceeding forty or fifty pounds a-year. The city priest, like the country priest, has neither rank nor power in the church. The only chance for an ambitious man is, that his wife may die; in which event he can take the vows, put on cowl and frock, obtain a career, become a fellow in the corporation of monks, and rise, if he be daring, supple, and adroit, to high places in his church.

That the parish priests are not content with their

position, is one of those open secrets in the church which every day become more difficult to keep. As married men, they feel that they are needlessly depressed in public esteem, and that the higher offices in the system should lie open to them no less than to the monks. Being many in number, rich in learning, intimate with the people, they ought to be strong in favour; yet through the craft of their Black rivals, they have been left, not only without the right of meeting, but without the means of making their voices heard. The peasant was never beaten down so low in the scale of life as his parish priest; for the serf had always his communal meeting, his choice of Elders, his right of speech, and his faculty of appeal. The parish priests expect a change; they expect it, not from within the clerical body, but from without; not from a Synod of monks, but from a married and reforming Tsar.

This change is coming on; a great and healing revolution; an act of emancipation for the working clergy, not less striking and beneficent than the act of emancipation for the toiling serfs.

CHAPTER XXIV.

A Conservative Revolution.

In the great conflict between monks and parish priests, the ignorant classes side with the monks, the educated classes with the parish priests.

The Black clergy, having no wives and children, stand apart from the world, and hold a doctrine hostile to the family spirit. Their rivals—though they have faults, from which the clergy in countries more advanced are free—are educated and social beings; and taking them man for man through all their grades, it is impossible to deny that the parish priests are vastly superior to the monks.

Yet the White clergy occupied (until 1869, the present year) a place in every way inferior to the Black. They were an isolated caste; they held no certain rank; they could not rise in the church; they exercised no power in her councils. Once a priest, a man was a priest for ever. A monk might live to be Rector, Archimandrite, Bishop, and Metropolite. Not so a married priest; the round of whose duty was confined to his parish work; to christening infants, to confessing women, to marrying lovers, to reading prayers for the dead, to saying mass, to collecting fees, and quarrelling with the peasants about his tithe. A monk directed his education; a monk appointed him to his cure of souls; a monk inspected his labour and loaded him with either praise or blame. A body of monks could drive him from his parish church; throw him into prison; utterly destroy the prospects of his life.

Great changes have been made in the present year; changes of deeper moment to the nation than anything effected in the Church since the reforms of Peter the Great.

This work of reform was started by the Emperor throwing open the clerical service to all the world, and putting an end to that customary succession of father and son as popes. Down to this year, the clergy has been a class apart—a sacred body—a Levitical order—in brief, a *caste*. Russia had her priestly families, like the Tartars and the Jews; and all the sons of a pope were bound to enter into the Church. This Oriental usage has been broken through. The clergy has been freed from a galling yoke, and the service has been opened to every one who may acquire the learning and enjoy the call. Young men, who would otherwise have been forced to take orders, will now be able to live by trade; the crowd of clerical idlers will melt away; and many a poor student with brains will be drawn into the spiritual ranks. This great reform is being carried forward, less by edicts which would fret the consciences of ignorant men, than by the application of general rules. To wit:—a question has arisen, whether, under this open system, the old rule of "once a priest, always a priest," holds good? It is a serious question, not for individuals only, but for the clerical society; and the monks have been moving heaven and earth to have their rule of "once a priest, always a priest" confirmed. But they have failed. No rule has been laid down in words, but a precedent has been laid down in fact.

Father Goumilef, a parish priest in the town of Riazan, applies for leave to give up his frock, and re-enter the world. Count Tolstoi, Minister of Education, and the Emperor's personal representative in the Holy Governing Synod, persuades that body to support Goumilef's prayer. On the 12th of November, (Oct. 31, o.s.)—a red-letter day henceforth in the Russian Calendar—the Emperor signs his release; allowing Goumilef to return from the clerical to the secular life. All his rights as a citizen are restored, and he is free to enter the public service in any province of the empire, save only that of Riazan, in which he has served the altar as a parish priest.

Connected with the abolition of caste came the new laws regulating the standing of a parish priest's children; laws conceived in a most gracious spirit. All sons of a parish priest are in future to rank as nobles; sons of a deacon are to be accounted gentlemen; sons of readers are to rank as burghers.

In his task of raising the parish clergy to a higher level, the reforming Emperor has found a tower of strength in Innocent, the noticeable man who occupies in Troitsa, the Archimandrite's chair, in Moscow, the Metropolite's throne.

Innocent passed his early years as a married priest in Siberia; doing, in the wild countries around the shores of Lake Baikal, genuine missionary work.

A noble wife went with him to and fro; Heaven blessed him with children; and the father learned how to speak with effect to sire and son. Thousands of converts blessed the devoted pair. At length the woman fainted by the way, and Innocent was left to mourn her loss; but not alone; their children remained to be his pride and stay.

When the Holy Governing Synod raised the missionary region of Irkutsk into a bishop's see, the crozier was forced upon Innocent by events. Already known as the Apostle of Siberia, the Synod could do little more than note the fact, and give him official rank. Of course, a mitre implied a cowl and gown; but Innocent, though his wife was dead, refused to become a monk. In stronger words than he was wont to use, he urged that the exclusion of married popes from high office in the priesthood, was a custom, not a canon, of his church. To every call from the monks, he answered that every man should be called to labour in the vineyard of the Lord according to his gifts. He yielded for the sake of peace; but though he took the vows, he held to his views on clerical celibacy, and the White clergy had now a bishop to whom they could look up as a worthy champion of their cause.

On the death of Philaret, two years ago, this friend of the White clergy was chosen by the Emperor to take his seat; so that now the actual Archimandrite of Troitsa, and Metropolite of Moscow, though he wears the cowl, is looked upon in Church society as a supporter of the married priests.

By happy chance, a first step had been taken

towards one great reform by Philaret, in raising to the chair of Rector of the Ecclesiastical Academy of Moscow a priest who was not a monk.

Forty miles to the north of Moscow, rises a table-land, on the edge of which is built a convent dedicated to the Holy Trinity, called in Russian Troitsa. This convent is said to be the richest in the world; not only in sacred dust and miraculous images, but in cups and coffers, in wands and crosses, in lamps and crowns. The shrine of St. Sergie, wrought in the purest silver, weighs a thousand pounds; and in the same cathedral with St. Sergie's shrine, there is a relievo of the Last Supper, in which all the figures, save that of Judas, are of finest gold. But these costly gauds are not the things which draw pilgrims to the Troitsa. They come to kneel before that Talking Madonna which, once upon a time, held speech with Serapion, a holy monk. They crowd round that portrait of St. Nicolas, which was struck by a shot from a Polish siege-gun, in the year of tribulation, when the Poles had made themselves masters of Moscow and the surrounding plains. They come still more to kiss the forehead of St. Sergie, the self-denying monk, who founded the convent, and blessed the banner of Dimitri, before that prince set forth on his campaign against the Tartar hordes on the Don. St. Sergie is the defence of his country, and his grave in the convent has never been polluted by the footprint of a foe. Often as Moscow fell, the Troitsa remained inviolate ground. The Tartars never reached it. Twice, if not more, the Poles advanced against it;

once with a mighty power; and the will to reduce it, cost them what lives it might. They lay before it sixteen months, and had to retire from before the walls at last. The French under Napoleon wished to seize it; and a body of troops was sent to the attack; but the saintly presence which had driven off the Poles was too much for the French. The troops returned, and the virgin convent stood.

These miracles of defence have given a vast celebrity to the saint, who has come to be thought, not only holy himself, but a cause of holiness in others. On the way from Moscow to Troitsa stands the hamlet of Hotkoff, in which lies the dust of Sergie's father and mother; over whose tombs a church and convent have been built. Every pilgrim on the road to Troitsa stops at this convent and adores their bones. "Have you been to Troitsa before?" we heard a pilgrim ask his fellow, as they trudged along the road. "Yes, thanks be to God." "Has Sergie given you what you came to seek?" "Well, no, not all." "Then you neglected to stop at Hotkoff, and adore his parents; he was angry with you." "Perhaps; God knows. It may be so. Next time, I will go to Hotkoff. Overlook my sin!" A railway has been made from Moscow to Troitsa; and the lazy herd of pilgrims go by train. The better sort still march along the dirty road, and count their beads in front of the wooden chapels and many rich crosses, as of old. St. Sergie has gained in wealth, and lost in credit by the convenience offered to pilgrims in the railway line.

In the centre of this fortress and sanctuary, the monks erected an Academy, in which priests were to be trained for their future work. A young man lives in it under Troitsa rule, and leaves it with the Troitsa brand. The Rector is a man of rank in the church; equal to the Master of Trinity among ourselves. Until the day when Philaret brought Father Gorski into office, his post had always been filled by an archimandrite. Now Father Gorski was a learned man, a good writer, and a great authority on points of church antiquity and ceremonial. Great in reputation, he was also advanced in years. Some objected to him on the ground that he was not a monk; but his fame as a learned man, his noticeable piety, and his nearness with the Metropolite, carried him through. Even the monks forgave him, when they found that he lived, like themselves, a secluded and cloistered life.

They hardly saw how much they were giving up in that early fight; for this man of monk-like habit had not taken vows; and in one of the strongholds of their power they were placing the education of their clergy in charge of a parish priest!

A second step in the line of march has been taken in the nomination of a married pope to the post of Rector of the Ecclesiastical Academy of St. Petersburg. Father Yanycheff is this new rector; and Father Yanycheff's wife is still alive. This call of a married man to such a chair has fired the church with hope and fear; the White clergy looking on it with surprise and joy, the Black clergy with amazement and despair.

Father Yanycheff—in whose person the fight is raging between these benedicts and celibates—is a young priest, who was educated in the Academy, until he took his degree of doctor, on which he was placed in the chair of theology at the University of St. Petersburg. In that chair, he became popular; his lectures being eloquent, his manners easy, and his opinions liberal. Some of the sleepy old prelates took alarm. Yanycheff, they said, was exciting his pupils; he was telling them to read and think; and the sleepy old prelates could see no good in such exercises of the brain. Reading and thinking lead men into doubt, and doubt is the plague by which souls are lost. They moved the Holy Governing Synod to interfere, and on the Synod interfering, the professor resigned his chair. Resolved on keeping his conscience free, he married, and accepted the office of pope in a city on the Rhine. His intellectual worth was widely known, and when, in process of time, a teacher was required for the young Princess Dagmar, a man skilful in languages and arts, as well as learned and liberal, Father Yanycheff was chosen for the task of preparing the imperial bride. The way in which he discharged his delicate office brought him into favour with the great; and on his return to his own country with the princess, Count Tolstoi got him appointed Rector of the Academy; a position of highest trust in the church; since it gives him a leading influence in the education of future popes.

The monks are all aghast; the Holy Governing Synod protests; and even the Metropolite refuses to recognise this act. But Count Tolstoi is firm; and the Synod knows but too well how the enemy stands at court. Yanycheff, on his side, has been prudent; and the wonder caused by his nomination is sensibly dying down. Meantime, people are getting used to the idea of a man with wife and child conducting the education of their future parish priests.

Once launched on a career of clerical reform, the court has moved with regular, if with cautious strides. All men can see that the first work to be done is to be done in the school-room and the college; for in Russia, as elsewhere, the teachers make the taught; and as the Rectors train the priests, ideas prevalent in the rectorial chairs will come in a few years to be the paramount views of the church.

A law has recently been passed by the Council of State, and promulgated by the Emperor, which deals the hardest blow yet suffered by the monks; a law taking away the right of nominating Rectors of Seminaries and Academies from the archbishops, and vesting it in a board of teachers and professors; subject only to approval—which may soon become a thing of course—by the higher spiritual powers. This law is opposed by all the convents and their chiefs; even Innocent, though friendly to the married clergy, stands, on this point, with his class.

A first election under this new law has just occurred in Moscow. When the law was published, Prof. Nicodemus, holding the chair of Rector in the Ecclesiastical Seminary of Moscow, sent in his resignation, on the ground that his position was become that of a Rector on sufferance. Every one felt that by resigning his chair, he was doing a noble thing; and if it had been possible for a monk to get a majority of votes in an open board, Nicodemus would, on that account, have been the popular choice. But no man wearing a cowl and gown had any chance. The contest lay between two married priests: Father Blagorazumof, a teacher in the Seminary, and Father Smirnof, editor of the Orthodox Review. Innocent took some part against Father Smirnof, whose writings he did not like; and Father Blagorazumof was elected to the vacant chair.

What has been done in Moscow will probably be done in other cities; so that in twenty years from the present time the education of youths for the ministry will have fallen entirely into the hands of married men.

The same principle of election has been applied to the appointment of Rural Deans. These officers were formerly named by the bishop, according to his sole will and pleasure. Now, by imperial order, they are elected by deputies from the parish priests.

CHAPTER XXV.

Secret Police.

THE new principle of referring things to a popular vote is coming into play on every side; nowhere in a form more striking than in the courts of law. Some twenty years ago the administration of justice was the darkest blot on Russian life.

What the Emperor had to meet and put away, on this side of his government, was a colossal evil.

In a country over which the prince has to rule as well as reign, a good many men must have a share in the exercise of irresponsible and imperial power—more perhaps than would have to divide the beneficent authority of a constitutional king. A prince has only two eyes, two ears, and two hands. The circle which he can see, and hear, and reach, is drawn closely round his person, and in all that he would do beyond that line, he must act through an intelligence other than his own; and for the blunders of this second self he has to bear the blame.

The parties who exercise this power in the imperial name, are the secret police and the provincial governors, general and local.

The secret police have an authority which knows no bounds, save that of the Emperor's direct command. They have a province of their own, apart from, and above, all other provinces in the state. Their chief, Count Shouvalof, is the first functionary of the empire; the only man who has a right of Audience by day and night. In Eastern nations rank is measured in no small degree by a person's right of access to the sovereign. Now, the right of audience in the Winter Palace is governed by the clearest rules. Ordinary ministers of the crown—Home Office, Education, Finance—can only see the Emperor once a-week. Greater ministers— War, and Foreign Affairs—can see him once a-day, but only at certain stated hours. A Minister of Police can walk into his cabinet any hour of the day, into his bed-room any hour of the night.

Not many years ago, the power of this minister was equal to his rank at court; in home affairs he was supreme; and many a poor ruler found himself at once his tool and dupe. Much of this power has now been lodged in courts of law, over which the police have no control; but over and beyond the law, a vast reserve is left with the police, who can still revise a sentence, and, as an "administrative measure," send a man into exile who has been acquitted by the courts.

While I was staying at Archangel, an actor and actress were brought from St. Petersburg in a tarantass, set down in the grass-grown square, near the poet's pedestal, and told to shift for themselves, though they were on no account to quit the town without the governor's pass. No one could tell what they had done. Their lips were closed; the newspapers were silent; but a thousand tongues were busy with their tale; and the likelier story seemed to be, that they had been playing a part in some drama of actual life. Clandestine marriages are not so rare in Russia as they are in England and the United States. Young princes love to run away with dancers, singers, and their like. Now these exiles in the north country were said to have been concerned in a runaway match, by which the pride of a powerful family had been stung; and since it was impossible to punish the offending parties, these poor artists had been whisked off their tinsel thrones, in order to appease a parent's wounded pride. The man and woman were not man and wife; but care for such loss of fame as a pretty woman might undergo by riding in a tarantass, day and night, twelve hundred versts, through a wild country, with a man who was not her spouse, seems never to have troubled the director of police. Stage heroines have no character in official eyes. There they were, in the north; and there they would have to stay, until the real offenders should be able to make their peace, whether they could manage to live in that city of trade, as honest folks should live, or not. Clever in their art, they opened a barn long closed, and the parlours of Archangel were agog with glee. What they performed could hardly be called a play. Two persons make a poor company, and these artists were of no high rank. They just contrived to keep their visitors awake by doing easy tricks in magic, and by acting short scenes from some of the naughtiest pieces in the world. It is to be hoped, on every ground, that the angry gods may be appeased, that the hero and heroine of this comedy may come back to the great city in which their talents are better known.

These actors were sent from the capital on a simple order from the police. They have not been tried; they have not been heard in defence; they have not been told the nature of their crime. An agent drove to their door in a drojki, asked to see So-and-so, and on going up, said, in tones which only the police can use, "Get ready; in three hours we start—for Archangel." Young or aged, male or female, the victim in such a case must snatch up what he can, follow his captor to the street, get into his drojki, and obey in silence the invisible powers. Not a word can be said in bar of his sentence; no court will open its doors to his appeal; no judge can hear his cry for help.

Their case is far from being a rare one. In the same streets of Archangel you meet a lady of middle age, who has been exiled from St. Petersburg on simple suspicion of being concerned in seducing students of the University from their allegiance to the country and the church.

Following in the wake of other changes, some reforms have been made in the Universities; made, on the whole, in a liberal and pacific sense. Nicolas put the students into uniform; hung swords in their belts; and gave them a certain standing in the public eye, as officers of the crown. They were his servants; and as his servants, they enjoyed some rights which they dearly prized. They ranked as nobles. They had their own police. They stood apart, as a separate corporation; and whether they sang through the street, or sat in the play-house, they appeared in public as a corporate body, and always in the front. But the reforming Emperor seeks to restore these civilian youths to the habits of civil life. Their swords have been hung up, their uniforms laid aside, their right of singing songs and damning plays in a body put away. All these distinctions are now abolished; and, like other civilians, the students have been placed under the city police and the ordinary courts.

These changes are unpopular with the students, who imagine that their dignity has been lessened by stripping them of uniform and sword; and some of these young men, professing all the while republican and communistic creeds, are clamouring for their class distinctions, and even hankering for the times when they were "servants of the Tsar."

In the month of March (1869) some noisy meetings of these young men took place. The Emperor heard of them, and sent for Trepof, his First Master of Police; a man of shrewd wit and generous temper, under whom the police have become all but popular. "What do these students want?" his Majesty began. "Two things," replied the Master, "bread and state." "Bread?" exclaimed the Emperor. "Yes," said the Master; "many of them are poor; with empty bellies, active brains, and saucy tongues."

"What can be done for them, poor fellows?"

"A few purses, Sire, would keep them quiet;

twenty thousand rubles now, and promise of a yearly grant in aid of poor students." "Let it be so," said the Prince.

These rubles were sent at once to the Rector and Professors to dispense, according to their knowledge of the students' needs; but, unluckily, the Rector and Professors treated the imperial gift as a bit of personal patronage, and they gave the purses to each other's sons and nephews, lads who could well afford to pay their fees. The students called fresh meetings, talked much nonsense, and drew up an Appeal to the People, written in a florid and offensive style.

Treating the government as an equal power, these madcaps printed what they called an ultimatum of four articles—(1) they demanded the right of establishing a Students' Club; (2) the right of meeting and addressing the government as a corporate body; (3) the control of all purses and scholarships given to poor students; (4) the abolition of university fees. Following these articles came an Appeal to the People for support against the minions of the Crown!

A party in the State—the enemies of reform—were said to have raised a fund for the purpose of corrupting these young men; and this party were suspected of employing the agency of clever women in carrying out their plans. It was not easy to detect these female plotters at their work, for the revolution they were trying to bring about was made with smiles and banter over cups of tea; but ladies were arrested in several streets, and the lady to be seen in Archangel was one of these victims; exiled on "suspicion" of having been concerned in printing the Appeal.

When she came into exile, every one was amazed; she seemed so weak and broken; she showed so little spirit; and when people talked with her, they found she had none of the talents necessary for intrigue. The comedy of government by "suspicion" stood confessed. Here was a prince, the idol of his country, armed in his mail of proof, surrounded by a million bayonets, not to speak of artillery, cavalry, and ships; and there was a frail creature, fifty years old, with neither beauty, followers, nor fortune to promote her views:—in such a foe, what could the Emperor be supposed to fear?

A young writer of some talent in St. Petersburg, one Dimitri Pisareff, was bathing in the sea, near his summer-house, and getting beyond his depth, was drowned. The young man was a politician, and having caused much scandal by his writings, he had passed some years in the fortress of St. Peter and St. Paul. Freed by the Emperor, he resumed his pen. After his death, Pavlenkoff, a bookseller in the city, who admired his talents, and thought he had served his country, opened a subscription among his readers for the purpose of erecting a stone above the young author's grave. The secret police took notice of the fact, and as Dimitri Pisareff was one of the names in their black list, they understood this effort to do him honour as a public censure of their zeal. Pavlenkoff is said to have been arrested in his shop, put into a cart, and with neither charge nor hearing, driven to the province of Viatka, twelve hundred versts from home. The shop is till open, and I believe the man has come back.

A more curious case is that of Gierst, a young novelist of mark, who began last year (1868) to publish in a monthly magazine, called Dielo, ("Business") a romance with the title of "Old Times." The opening chapters showed that his tale was likely to be clever; bold in thought and brilliant in style. Gierst took the part of Young Russia against Old Russia, and his chapters were devoured by youths in all the colleges and schools. Every one began to talk of the story, and to discuss the questions raised by it—men and things in the past, in contrast with the hopes and talents of the present reign. The police took part with the elders; and when the novelist who made the stir could not be answered with argument, they silenced him by a midnight call. An officer came to his lodgings with the usual order to depart at once. Away sped the horses, he knew not whither; driving on night and day, until they arrived at Totma, one of the smaller towns in the province of Vologda, nine hundred versts from St. Petersburg. There he was tossed out of his cart, and told to remain until fresh orders came from the Minister of Police.

None of Gierst's friends, at first, knew where he was. His rooms in St. Petersburg were empty; he had gone away: and the only trace which he had left behind was the tale of a domestic, who had seen him carried off. No one dared to ask about him. Reference to him in the journals was forbidden; and the public only learned from the non-appearance of his story in the "Dielo" that the police had somehow interfered with the free exercise of his pen. The letters which he wrote to the papers were laid aside, as being too dangerous for the public eye; and it was only by a ruse that he conveyed to his readers the knowledge of his whereabouts.

Gierst sent to the editor of "Dielo" a letter of apology for the interruption of his tale. He merely said it would not be carried farther for the present; and the police raised no objection to the publication of this letter in "Dielo." They overlooked the date which the letter bore; and the one word "Totma" told the public all.

The world enjoyed a laugh at the police; and the irritated officials tried to vent their rage on the young wit who had proved that they were fools. Gierst remains an exile at Totma, and the public still awaits the story from his hands. But a thousand novels, rich in art and red in spirit, could not have touched the public conscience like the haunting memory of this unfinished tale.

CHAPTER XXVI.

Provincial Rulers.

Russia is divided into provinces, each of which is ruled by a governor and a vice-governor named by the crown.

A dozen years ago, the governor and his lieutenant was each a petty Tsar; doing what he pleased in his department; and answering only now and then, like a Turkish pasha, by forfeiture of office, for the public good. Charged with the maintenance of public order, he was armed with a power as terrible as that of the imperial police; the right to suspect his neighbour of discontent, and act on this bare suspicion as though the fault were proved in a court of law. In England and the United States, the word Suspicion has lost its use, and well-nigh lost its sense. Our officers of police are not permitted to "suspect" a thief. They must either take him in the fact, or leave him alone. From Calais to Perm, however, the word "suspicion" is still a name of fear; for in all the countries lying between the English Channel and the Ural Mountains, "ordre supérieur" is a force to which rights of man and courts of law must equally give way.

The governor, or vice-governor, of a Russian province, representing his sovereign lord, might find, or fancy that he found, some reason to suspect a man of disaffection to the crown. He might be wrong, he might even be absurdly wrong. The man might be loyal as himself; might even be in a position to prove that loyalty in open court; and yet his innocence would avail him nothing. Proofs are idle when the courts are not open to appeal, and judges have no power to hear the facts. "Done by superior orders," was the answer to all cries and protests. A resistless power was about his feet, and he was swept away by a force from which there was no appeal; not even to the ruling prince; and the victim of an erring, perhaps a malicious, governor, had no resource against the wrong, except in resignation to what might seem to be the will of God.

The men who could use and abuse this terrible power were many. Russia is divided into forty-nine provinces, besides the kingdom of Poland, the Grand Duchy of Finland, the Empire of Siberia, the khanates and principalities of the Caucasus. In these forty-nine provinces, the governors and vice-governors had the power to exile anybody on mere suspicion of political discontent. In other regions of the empire, this power was even more diffused than it was in the purely Russian districts. Taking all the Russias in one mass, there can hardly have been less than two hundred men (excluding the police) who could seize a citizen in the name of public order, and condemn him, unheard, to live in any part of the empire, from the Persian frontiers to the Polar Sea.

The Princess V . . . . ., a native of Podolia, young, accomplished, wealthy, was loved by all her friends, adored by all the young men of her province. One happy youth possessed her heart, and this young man was worthy of the fortune he had won. Their days of courtship passed, and they were looking forward to the day when they would wear together their sacred crowns; but then an unseen agent crossed their path and broke their hearts. Some days before their betrothal should have taken place, an officer of police appeared at the lover's door, with a peremptory order for him to quit Poltava for the distant government of Perm. Taken from his house at a moment's notice, he was hurried to the general office of police, where his papers were made out, and being put into a common cart, he was whisked away in the company of two gendarmes. A month was occupied in his journey; two or three months elapsed before his friends in Podolia knew that he was safe. He found a friend in the mountain town; by whom his life as an exile was made a little less rugged than it might have been. An advocate was won for him at court; the senate was moved, though cautiously, in his behalf; and at the end of two years, his tormentor was persuaded to relax his grip. But though he was suffered to leave his place of banishment, he was forbidden to return to his native town.

The Princess kept her faith to him: staying in Podolia while he was still at Perm; living down the suspicions in which they were both involved; and joined him at St. Petersburg so soon as he got leave to enter that city. There they were married; and there I met them in society. Not a cloud is on their fame. They are free to go and come; except that they must not live in their native town. No power save that which sent the bridegroom into exile can recall them to their home. Yet down to this hour, the gentleman has never been able to ascertain the nature of his offence.

In time, the country will free herself from this Asiatic abuse of power. With bold, but cautious hand, the Emperor has felt his way. His governors of provinces have been told to act with prudence; not to think of sending men into exile unless the case is flagrant; and only then after reference of all the facts to St. Petersburg.

Some dozen years ago, before the new reforms had taken hold, and officers in the public service had come to count on the appeal being heard, a case occurred which allows one to give, in the form of an anecdote, a picture of the evils now being slowly rooted out. Count A. . . . a young vice-governor, fresh from college, came to live in a certain town of the Black Soil country. Fond of dogs and horses, fond of wines and dinners, the young gentleman found his official income far below his wants. He took "his own" (what Russian officials used to call vzietka), from every side; for he loved to keep his house open, his stable full, his card-room merry; and a nice house, a good stable, and a merry card-room, cost a good many rubles in the year. He was lucky with his cards; luckier, some losers said, than a perfectly honest player should be; yet the two ends of his income and his out-go never could be made to meet.

The Treasurer of the town was Andrew Ivanovitch Gorr; a man of peasant birth, who had been sent to college, and after taking a good degree, had been put into the Civil Service; where, by his soft ways, his patient deference to those above him, and his perfect loyalty to his trust, he had risen to the post of treasurer in this provincial town.

The Count called Andrew into his chamber, and bade him, with a careless gesture, pay a small debt for him. Andrew bowed, and waited for the rubles. The Count just waived him off; but seeing that Andrew would not take the hint, he said: "Yes, yes, pay the debt; we will arrange it in the afternoon." Then Andrew paid the money, and in less than a week he was asked to pay again. From week to week he went on paying, with due submission to his chief, but with an inward doubt as to whether this paying of private debts with public money would turn out well. Twice or thrice the Count named a day when the money which he was taking from the public coffers should be replaced. In the meantime the debt was every week increasing in amount; so that the Provincial chest was all but drained, to pay the vice-governor's personal debts.

Andrew was in despair, for the day was fast coming round when the Imperial auditors would come to revise his books, and count the money in his box. Unless the fund was restored before they came, he would be lost; for the balance was in his charge, and the Count could hardly cover his default. On Andrew telling his wife what he had been drawn by his habit of obeying orders into doing, he was urged by that sage adviser to go at once to the vice-governor and beg him to replace the cash before the auditors arrived.

"The auditors will come next week?" asked A.... "All will be well. I will send a messenger to my estates. In five days he will come back, and the money shall be paid. Prepare a draft of the account, and bring it to my house, with the proper receipt and seal."

On the fifth day the auditors arrived, a little before their time; and being eager to push on, they named the next morning, at ten o'clock, for going into the accounts. The Treasurer ran to the palace, and saw the Count in his public room, surrounded by his secretaries. "It is well," he said to Andrew, with his pleasant smile; "the messenger has come back with the money; bring the paper and the receipt to my smoking-room at ten o'clock to night, and we'll put the account to rights."

Andrew was at his door by ten o'clock with the statement of his debts, and a receipt for the money. "Yes," said the Count, dropping his eye down the line of figures, "the account is just:—fifteen thousand seven hundred rubles. Let me look at the receipt. Yes, that is well drawn. You deserve to be promoted, Andrew! Talents like yours are lost in a provincial town. You ought to be a minister of state! Oblige me by asking my man to come in."

A servant entered.

"Go up to the Madame, and ask her if she can come downstairs for a moment," said the Count. The servant slipped away, and the Count, while waiting for his return, made many jokes and pleasantries, so that the time ran swiftly past. He kept the papers in his hand.

When Andrew saw that it was near eleven o'clock, he ventured to ask if the man was not long in coming. "Long!" exclaimed the vice-governor, starting up, "an age. Where can the fellow be? He must have fallen asleep on the stairs."

Going out of the room in search of him, the Count closed the door behind him, saying, "Wait a few minutes,—I will go myself." Andrew sat still as a stone. He noticed that the Count had taken with him the schedule of debts and the signed receipt. He felt uneasy in his mind. He stared about the room, and counted the beatings of the clock. His head grew hot; his heart was beating with a throb that could be heard. No other sound broke the night; and when he opened the door and put his ear to the passage, the silence seemed to him like that of a crypt.

The clock struck twelve.

Leaping up from his stupor, he banged the door and shouted up the stairs, but no one answered him; and snatching a fearful daring from his misery, he ran along several corridors until he tripped and fell over a man in a great fur cloak. "Get up, and show me to the vice-governor's room," said Andrew fiercely; on which the domestic shook his cloak, and rubbed his eyes. "The vice-governor's room?" "Yes, fellow; come, be quick." The man led him back to the chamber he had left; which was, in fact, the private reception room. "Stay here, and I will seek him." Shortly the man returned with news that his master was in bed. "In bed!" cried Andrew, more and more excited; "go to him again, and ask him if he has forgotten me. Tell him I am waiting his return." A minute later, he came back to say the Count was fast asleep, and that his valet dared not wake him for the world. "Asleep!" groaned the poor treasurer; "you must awake him. I cannot leave without seeing him. It is the Emperor's service, and will not wait."

At the Emperor's name, the servant said he would try again. An hour of misery went by, before he came to say the Count was in bed, and would not see him. If he had business to transact he must come another day, and at the reception hour.

In a moment Andrew was at the Count's door, and in his room, to which the noise brought up a dozen people. "What is this tumult all about?" frowned the Count, rising sharply in his bed. "Tumult!" cried Andrew, waxing hot with terror; "I want the rubles." "Rubles!" said the Count, with feigned astonishment; "what rubles do you mean?" "The rubles we have taken from the provincial coffer." "That we have taken from the coffer! We? What we? What rubles? Go to bed, man, and forget your dreams."

"Then give me back my paper and receipt."

"Paper and receipt!" said the Count, with affected pity; "look to him well. See him safe home; and tell his wife to watch that he does not wander in his sleep. He might fall into the river in such fits. Look to him;" and the vice-governor fell back upon his pillow as the servants bowed.

Put to the door, and left to seek his way, the treasurer felt that he was lost. The Count, he saw, would swear and forswear. Even if he confessed his fault to the auditors, telling them how he had been persuaded against his duty, the Count could produce his receipt in proof that the funds had been repaid.

Going back to his office, he sat down on a stool, and after looking at his books and papers once again, to see that the whole night's work was not a dream, as the Count had said, he took up his pen and wrote a history of his affairs.

Restless in her bed, his wife got up to seek him; and knowing that he was busy with his accounts, and would be likely to stay late with his chief, she went into his office, where the light was burning dimly on the desk—to find him hanging from a beam. Piercing the air with her cries, she brought in a crowd of people, some of whom cut down the body, while others ran for the doctor. He was dead.

Like an Oriental, he killed himself in order that, in his death, he might punish the man whom he could not touch in life.

The paper which he left on his desk was open, and as many persons saw it in part, and still more knew of its existence, the matter could not be hushed up, even though the vice-governor had been twenty times a Count. The people cried for justice on the culprit; and by orders from St. Petersburg the Count was relieved of his office, arrested on the charge of abusing a public trust, and placed on his defence before a Secret Commission in the town over which he had lately reigned.

The Emperor, it is said, was anxious to send him to the mines, from which so many nobler men had recently come away; but the interest of his family was great at court; the Secret Commission was a friendly one; and he escaped with the sentence of perpetual dismissal from the public service —not a light sentence to a man who is at once a beggar and a count.

Alexander, feeling for the widow of his dead servant, ordered the pension which would have been due to her husband to be paid to her for life.

CHAPTER XXVII.

Open Courts.

OFFENCES like those of Count A . . . (some twelve years old), in which a great offence was proved, yet justice was defeated more than half, in spite of the imperial wishes, led the Council of State into considering how far it would be well to replace the Secret Commissions by regular Courts of Law.

The public benefits of such a change were obvious. Justice would be done, with little or no respect to persons; and the Emperor would be relieved from his direct and personal action in the punishment of crime. But what the public gained, the circles round the prince were not unlikely to lose; and these court circles raised a cry against this project of reform. "The obstacles," they said, "were vast. Except in Moscow and St. Petersburg, no lawyers could be found; the code was cumbrous and imperfect; and the public was unprepared for such a change. If it was difficult to find judges, it was impossible to find jurors." Listening to every one, and weighing facts, the Emperor held his own. He got reports drawn up; he won his opponents over one by one; and in 1865 the Council of State was ready with a volume of legal reform, as vast and noble as his plan for emancipating serfs.

Courts of justice were to be opened in every province; and all these courts of justice were to be public courts. Trained judges were to preside. The system of written evidence was abolished. A prisoner was to be charged in a formal act; he was to see the witnesses face to face; he was to have the right, in person or by his counsel, of questioning those witnesses on points of fact. A jury was to decide the question of guilt or innocence. The judges were to be paid by the crown, and were on no pretext whatever to receive a fee. A juror was to be a man of means; a trader, a well-off peasant, an officer of not less than five hundred rubles a-year. A majority of jurors was to decide.

The Imperial Code was brought into harmony with these new methods of procedure. Capital punishment—already abolished for civil crimes—was abolished for military crimes in time of peace; Archangel and the Caucasus were substituted for the mines. The Tartar punishments of beating, flogging, running the ranks, were stopped at once; and every branch of criminal treatment was brought up —in theory, at least—to the level of England and the United States.

Term by term, this new system of trial by judge and jury, instead of by secret commissions, is now being introduced into all the larger towns. I have watched the working of this new system in several provinces; but give an account, by preference, of a trial in a new court, in a new district, under circumstances which put the virtues of a jury to some local strain.

Dining one evening with a friend in Rostof, on the Lower Don, I find myself seated next to President Gravy, to whom I am introduced by our common host as an English barrister and Justice of the Peace. The assize is sitting, and as a curious case of child exposure is coming on next day, about the facts of which provincial feeling is much excited, President Gravy offers me a seat in his court.

This court is a new court, opened in the present year; a moveable court, consisting of a President and two assistant judges; sitting in turn at Taganrog, Berdiansk, and Rostof; towns between which there is a good deal of rivalry in business, often degenerating into local strife. The female accused of exposing her infant comes from a Tartar village near Taganrog; and as no good thing was ever known to come from the district of Taganrog, the voice of Rostof has condemned this female, still untried, to a felon's doom.

Next morning, we are in court by ten o'clock; a span-new chamber, on which the paint is not yet dry; with a portrait of the imperial law-reformer hung above the judgment-seat. A long hall is parted into three portions by a daïs and two silken cords. The judges, with the clerk, and public prosecutor, sit on the daïs, at a table; and the citizens of Rostof occupy the benches on either wing. In front of the daïs sit the jurors, the short-hand writer (a young lady), the advocates and witnesses; and near these latter stands the accused woman, attended by a civil officer of the court. Nothing in the room suggests the idea of feudal state and barbaric power. President Gravy wears no wig, no robe; nothing but a golden chain, and the pattern civilian's coat. No halberts follow him, no mace and crown are borne before him. He enters by the common door. A priest in his robes of office stands beside a book and cross; he is the only man in costume, as the advocates wear neither wig nor gown. No soldier is seen; and no policeman except the officer in charge of the accused. There is no dock; the prisoner stands or sits as she is placed; her back against the wall. If violence is feared, the judges order in a couple of soldiers, who stand on either side the prisoner holding their naked swords; but this precaution is seldom used. An open gallery is filled with persons who come and go all day, without disturbing the court below.

President Gravy, the senior judge, is a man of forty-five. The son of a captain of gendarmerie in Odessa, he took by choice to the profession of advocate, and after three years' practice in the courts of St. Petersburg, he was sent to the new Azof circuit. His assistant judges are younger men.

President Gravy opens his court; the priest asks a blessing; the jurors are selected from a panel; the prisoner is told to stand forth; and the indictment is read by the clerk. A keen desire to see the culprit and to hear the details of her crime has filled the benches with a better class than commonly attends the court, and many of the Rostof ladies flutter in the gayest of morning robes. The case is one to excite the female heart.

Anna Kovalenka, eighteen years of age, and living, when at home, in a village on the Sea of Azof, is tall, elastic, dark, with ruddy complexion, and braided hair bound up in a crimson scarf. Some Tartar blood is in her veins; and the young woman is the ideal portrait of a Bokhara bandit's wife. A motherly old creature stands by her side; an aunt, her mother being long since dead. Her father is a peasant, badly off, with five girls; this Anna eldest of the five.

Her case is, that she had a lover, that she bore a child, that she concealed the birth, and that her infant died. In her defence, it is alleged, according to the manners of her country, that her lover was a man of her own village, not a stranger; one of those governing points which, on the Sea of Azof, make a young woman's amours right or wrong. So far, it is assumed, no fault is fairly to be charged. Her child was born and died; the facts are not disputed; but the defendants urge, in explanation, that she was very young in years; that her couching was very hard; that milk-fever set in, with loss of blood and wandering of the brain; that the young mother was helpless, that the infant was neglected unconsciously, and that it died.

Very few persons in the court appear inclined to take this view; but those who take it feel that the lover of this girl is far more guilty than the girl herself; and they ask each other why the seducer is not standing at her side to answer for his life. His name is known; he is even supposed to be in court. Gospodin Lebedeff, the Public Prosecutor, has done his best to include him in the criminal charge; but he is foiled by the woman's love and wit. By the Imperial Code, the fellow cannot be touched, unless she names him as the father of her child; and all Lebedeff's appeals and menaces are thrown away upon her; this heroine of a Tartar village baffling the veteran lawyer's arts with a steadiness worthy of a better cause and a nobler man.

The first witness called is a peasant woman from the village in which Anna Kovalenka lives. She is not sworn in the English way; the court having been put, as it were, under sacred obligations by the priest; but the bench instructs her as to the nature of evidence, and enjoins her to speak no word that is not true. She says, in few and simple words, she found the dead body; she carried it into Anna's cabin; the young woman admitted that the child was hers; and, on further questions, that she had concealed the birth. She gives her evidence quietly, in a breathless court; her neighbour standing near her all the while, and the judge assisting her by questions now and then. The audience sighs when she stands down; her evidence being full enough to send the prisoner to Siberia for her natural life.

The second witness is a doctor; bland, and fat, and scientific; the witness on whose evidence the defence will lie. A quickened curiosity is felt as the fat and fatherly man, with big blue spectacles and kindly aspect, rises, bows to the bench, and enters into a long and delicate report on the maladies under which females suffer in and after the throes of labour, when the regular functions of mind and body have been deranged by a sudden call upon the powers reserved by nature for the sustenance of infant life. A buzz of talk on the ladies' bench is speedily put down by a tinkle of President Gravy's bell. The judges put minute and searching questions to this witness; but they make no notes of what he says in answer; the general purpose of which is to show that the first medical evidence picked up by the police was defective; that a woman in the situation of Anna, poor, neglected, inexperienced, might conceal her child without intending to do it harm, and might cause it to die of cold without being morally guilty of its death. Two or three questions are put to him by Lebedeff, and then the kindly, fat, old gentleman wipes his spectacles and drops behind.

Lebedeff deals in a lenient spirit with the case. The facts, he says (in effect), are strong, and tell their own tale. This woman bears a child; she conceals the birth; this concealment is a crime. She puts her child away in a secret place; her child is found dead—dead of hunger and neglect. Who can doubt that she exposed and killed this child in order to rid herself at once of her burthen and her shame? "The crime of child-murder is so common in our villages," he concludes, "that it cries to heaven against us. Let all good men combine to put it down, by a rigorous execution of the law."

Gospodin Tseborenko, a young advocate from

Taganrog, sent over specially to conduct the defence, replies by a brief examination of the facts; contending that his client is a girl of good character, who has never had a lover beyond her village, and is not likely to have committed a crime against nature. He suggests that her child may have been dead at the birth—that in her pain and loneliness, not knowing what she was about, and never dreaming about the Code, she concealed the dead body from her father's eyes. Admitting that infant murder is the besetting sin of villagers in the south of Russia, he contends that the children put away are only such as the villagers consider things of shame—that is to say, the offspring of their women by strangers and men of rank.

President Gravy rings his bell—the court is all alert—and, after a brief presentment of the leading points to the jury, who on their side listen with grave attention to every word, he puts three several queries into writing:—

I. Whether in their opinion Anna Kovalenka exposed her child with a view to kill it?

II. Whether, if she did not in their opinion expose it with a view to kill it, she wilfully concealed the birth?

III. Whether, if she either knowingly exposed and killed her child, or wilfully concealed the birth, there were any circumstances in the case which call for mitigation of the penalties provided by the Penal Code?

The sheet of paper on which he writes these queries is signed by the three judges, and handed over to the foreman, who takes it and retires with his brethren of the jury to find as they shall see fit.

While the trial has been proceeding, Anna Kovalenka has been looking on with patient unconcern—neither bold nor timid—but with a look of resignation singular to watch. Only once she kindled into spirit; that was when the peasant woman was describing how she found the body of her child. She smiled a little when her advocate was speaking; only a faint and vanishing smile. Lebedeff seemed to strike her as something sacred; and she listened to his not unkindly speech as she might have listened to a sermon by her village priest.

In twenty minutes the jury comes into court with their finding written by the foreman on the sheet of paper given to him by the judge. President Gravy rings his bell, and bids the foreman read his answer to the first query.

"No!" says the foreman in a grave, loud voice. The audience starts, for this is the capital charge.

To the second query, "No!"

"That is enough," says the judge; and turning to the woman, he tells her in a tender voice that she has been tried by her country and acquitted, that she is now a free woman, and may go and sit down among her friends and neighbours.

Now for the first time she melts a little; shrinks behind the policeman; snatches up the corner of her gown; and steadying herself in a moment, wipes her eyes, kisses her aunt, and creeps away by a private door.

Everybody in this court has done his duty well, the jurors best of all; for these twelve men, who never saw an open court in their lives until the current year, have found a verdict of acquittal in accordance with the facts, but in the teeth of local prejudice, bent on sending the woman from Taganrog to the mines for life.

What schools for liberty and tolerance have been opened in these courts of law!

CHAPTER XXVIII.

Islam.

KAZAN is the point where Europe and Asia meet. The paper frontiers lie a hundred miles farther east, along the crests of the Ural Mountains and the banks of the Ural river; but the actual line on which the Tartar and the Russian stand face to face, on which mosque and church salute the eye together, is that of the Lower Volga, flowing through the Eastern Steppe, from Kazan to the Caspian Sea. This frontier line lies eastward of Bagdad.

Kazan, a colony of Bokhara, an outpost of Khiva, was not very long ago the seat of a splendid khanate; and she is still regarded by the fierce and languid Asiatics as the western frontier of their race and faith. In site and aspect this old city is extremely fine, especially when the floods run high, and the swamps beneath her walls become a glorious lake. A crest of hill—which poets have likened to a wave, a keel, and a stallion's back—runs parallel to the stream. This crest is the Kremlin, the strong place, the seat of empire; scarped, and walled, and armed; the battlements crowned with gateways, towers, and domes. Beyond the crest of hill, inland from the Volga, runs a fine plateau, on which stand remnants of rich old courts and towers; a plateau somewhat bare, though brightened—here and there—by garden, promenade, and chalet. Under this ridge lies Kaban Lake, a long, dark sheet of water, on the banks of which are built the business quarters, in which the craftsmen labour and the merchants buy and sell; a wonderfully busy and thriving town. Each quarter has a character of its own. The Kremlin is Christian; the High Street Germanesque. A fine old Tartar gateway, called the Tower of Soyonbeka, stands in front of the cathedral; but much of the citadel has been built since the Khanate fell before the troops of Ivan the Fourth. Down in the lower city, by the Kaban Lake, dwell the children of Islam, the descendants of Batu Khan, the countrymen of the Golden horde.

The birthplace of these Tartar nations was the Eastern Steppe; their line of march was the Volga bank; and their affections turn still warmly to their ancient seats. The names of Khiva and Bokhara sound to a Tartar as the names of Shechem and Jerusalem sound to a Jew. In his poetry these countries are his ideal lands. He sings to his mistress of the groves of Bokhara; he compares her cheek to the apples of Khiva; and he tells her the fervour of his passion is like the summer heat of Balkh.

An Arab legend puts into the Prophet's mouth a saying, which is taken by his children as a promise, that in countries where the palm-trees bear fruit his followers should possess the land; but that in countries where the palm-trees bear no fruit, though they might be dwellers for a time, the land would never be their own. The promise, if it were a promise, has been kept in the spirit for a thousand years. No date-bearing country known to the Arabs defied their arms; from no date-bearing country, once over-run, have they been yet dislodged. When Islam pushed her out-posts beyond the line of palms, as in Spain and Russia, she had to fall back, after her trial of strength on the colder fields, into her natural zones. As she fell back from Granada on Tangiers and Fez, so she retired from Kazan on Khiva and Bokhara; a most unwilling retreat, the grief of which she assuaged in some degree by passionate hope of her return. The Moors, expecting to reconquer Seville and Granada, keep the keys of their ancient palaces, the title-deeds of their ancient lands in Spain. The Kirghiz, also, claim the lands and houses of their countrymen, and the Kirghiz khan describes himself as lineal heir to the reigning princes of Kazan. In the East, as in the West, the children of Islam look on their present state as a correction laid upon them by a father for their faults. Some day they trust to find fresh favour in his sight. The term of their captivity may be long; but it will surely pass away, and when the Compassionate yields in his mercy, they will return in triumph to their ancient homes.

In the meantime it is right to mark the different spirit in which the vanquished sons of Islam have been treated in the West and in the East. From

Granada every Moor was driven by fire and sword; for many generations no Moor was suffered to come back into Spain, under pain of death. In Russia the Tartars were allowed to live in peace; and after forty years they were allowed to trade in the city which had formerly been their own. No doubt there have been fierce and frequent persecutions of the weaker side in these countries; for the great conflict of Cross and Crescent has grown into a second nature, equally with the Russian and Tartar, and the rivalries which once divided Moscow and Kazan still burn along the Kirghiz Steppe. The capitals may be farther off, but the causes of enmity are not removed by space and time. The Cross is at St. Petersburg and Kief, the Crescent at Bokhara and Khiva; but between these points there is a sympathy and an antipathy, like that which fights between the two magnetic poles. The Tartars have captured Nijni and Moscow, many times; the Russians will some day plant their standards on the Tower of Timour Beg.

A man who walks through the Tartar town in Kazan, admiring the painted houses, the handsome figures, the Oriental garbs, the graceful minarets, can hardly help feeling that these children of Islam hold their own with a grace and dignity worthy of a prouder epoch. "Given to theft and eating horseflesh," is the verdict of a Russian officer; "otherwise not so bad." "Your servants seem to be Tartar?" "Yes; the rascals make good servants; for, look you, they never drink; and when they are trusted they never steal." In all the great houses of St. Petersburg and Moscow, and in the large hotels everywhere, we have Tartar servants, chosen on account of their sobriety and honesty. The Begs and Mirzas fled from the country when their city was stormed, and only the craftsmen and shepherds remained behind; yet a new aristocracy of trade and learning has sprung up; and the titles of Mirza and mollah are now enjoyed by men whose grandfathers held the plough. These Tartars of Kazan are better schooled than their Russian neighbours; most of them can read, write, and cypher; and their youths are in high demand as merchants, salesmen, and bankers' clerks; offices of trust in which, with care and patience, they are sure to rise. Mirza Yunasoff, Mirza Burnaief, and Mirza Apakof, three of the richest traders in the province, are self-made men. No one denies them the rank of Mirza (lord, or prince). Mirza Yunasoff has built, at his private charge, a mosque and school.

It is very hard for a Christian to get any sort of clue to the feelings of these sober and industrious folk. That they value their religion more than their lives is easy to find out; but whether they share the dreams of their brethren in Khiva and Bokhara is not known. Meanwhile they work and pray, grow rich and strong. An innocent and useful body in the empire, they are wisely left alone, so far as they can be left alone.

They cannot, however, be treated as of no importance in the state. They are of vast importance; not as enemies only, but as enemies camped on the soil, and drawing their supports from a foreign land. Even those among the Tartars who are least excited by events around them, feel that they are out of their natural place. They hate the Cross. They are Asiatics; with their faces and affections turning day and night, not towards Moscow and St. Petersburg, but towards Khiva, Bokhara, and Samarcand. A foreign city is their holy place, a foreign ruler their anointed chief. They get their mollahs from Bokhara, and they wait for conquerors from the Kirghiz steppes. They have not learned to be Russians, and they will not learn; so that, whether the Government wishes it or not, the conflict of race and creed will rage through the coming years, even as it has raged through the past.

Reforming the country on every side, the Emperor is not neglecting this Eastern point; and in the spirit of all his more recent changes, he is taking up a new position as regards the Tartar race and creed. Nature and policy combine to prevent him trying to convert the Mussulmans by force; but nothing prevents him from trying to draw them over by the moral agencies of education and humanity. Feeling that where the magistrate would fail, the teacher may succeed, the Emperor is opening schools in his Eastern provinces, under the care of Professor Ilminski, a learned Russian, holding the chair of Tartar Languages and Literature in the University of Kazan. These schools already number twenty-four, of which the one near Kazan is the chief and model.

Professor Ilminski drives me over to these Tartar schools. We visit a school for boys, and a school for girls; for the sexes are kept apart, in deference to Oriental notions about the female sex. The rooms are clean and well kept; the children neat in dress, and orderly in manner. They are taught by young priests especially trained for the office, and learn to sing, as well as to read and cypher. Books are printed for them in Russian type, and a Tartar press is working in connexion with the University. This printing of books, especially of the Psalms and Gospels, in the Tartar tongue, is doing much good; for the natives of Kazan are a pushing and inquisitive people, fond of reading and singing; and the poorest people are glad to have good books brought to their doors, in a speech that every one can hear and judge for himself. In the same spirit the Emperor has ordered mass to be said in the Tartar tongue; a wise and thoughtful step; a hint, it may be, to the mollahs, who have not come to see, and never may come to see, that any other idioms than Arabic and Persian should be used in their mosques. If these clever traders and craftsmen of Kazan are ever to be converted from Islam to Christianity, they must be drawn over in these gentle ways, and not by the jailor's whip and the Kozak's brand.

The children sing a psalm; their bright eyes gleaming at the sound. They sing in time and tune; but in a fierce, marauding style, as though the anthem were a bandit's stave.

Not much fruit has yet been gathered from this field. "Have you any converts from the better classes?" "No; not yet," the Professor sighs; "the citizens of Kazan are hard to win; but we get some little folk from villages on the steppe, and train them up in the fear of God. Once they are with us, they can never turn back."

Such is the present spirit of the law. A Moslem may become a Christian; a Christian may not become a Moslem; and a convert who has taken upon himself the cross can never legally lay it down. It is an Eastern, not a Western rule; and while it remains in force, the Cross will be denied the use of her noblest arms. Not until conscience is left to work in its own way, as God shall guide it, free from all fear of what the police may rule, will the final victory lie with the faith of Christ.

Shi Abu Din, chief mollah of Kazan, receives me in Asiatic fashion; introduces me to two brother mollahs, licensed to travel as merchants; and leads me over the native colleges and schools. This mollah, born in a village near Kazan, was sent to the University of Bokhara, in which city he was trained for his labours among the Moslems living on Russian soil, just as our Puritan clergy used to seek their education in Holland, our Catholic clergy in Spain. Shi Abu Din is considered, even by the Professor of Tartar languages, as a learned and upright man. His swarthy brethren have just arrived from Bokhara, by way of the Kirghiz Steppe. They tell me the roads are dangerous, and the countries lying east of the Caspian Sea disturbed. Still the roads, though closed to the Russians, are open to caravan merchants, if they know the dialects and ways of men. No doubt they are open to mollahs travelling with caravans through friendly tribes.

The Tartars of Kazan are, of course, polygamists; so that their social life is as much unlike the Russian as their religious life.

CHAPTER XXIX.

The Volga.

From Kazan to the Caspian Sea, the Volga flows between Islam and Christendom. One small town, Samara, has been planted on the eastern bank; a landing place for Orenburg and the Kirghiz Steppe. All other towns—Simbirsk, Volsk, Saratof, Tsaritzin—rise on the western bank, and look across the river towards the Ural ridge. Samara is a Kirghiz, rather than a Russian town, and but for the military posts, and the traffic brought along the military roads, the place would be wholly in Moslem hands. Samara has a name in the East, as a place for invalids; the cure being wrought by means of fermented mare's milk, the diet and medicine of rovers on the Tartar steppe.

A Christian settlement of the Volga line from Kazan to the Caspian Sea must be a work of time. Three hundred and seventeen years have passed since Ivan the Terrible stormed Kazan; three hundred and twelve years since his armies captured Astrakhan, and opened a passage through Russia to the Caspian Sea; yet the Volga is a frontier river to this very hour; and it is not too much to say, that the noblest watercourse in Europe is less familiar to English merchants in Victoria's time than it was in Elizabeth's time.

The first boats which sailed the Volga, from her upper waters to her mouth, were laden with English goods. So soon as Challoner found a way up the Dvina, a body of merchants formed themselves into a society for discovering unknown lands, and this body of London merchants was the means of opening up Eastern Russia to the world.

The man who first struck the Volga was Anthony Jenkinson, agent of these discoverers, who brought out a cargo of cottons and kerseys, ready dyed and dressed, of lead and tin for roofing churches, and a vast assortment of pewter pots; all of which his masters in London expected him to exchange for the gums and silks, the gold and pearls, of mythical Cathay. Coming from the Frozen Sea, he noticed with a trader's eye that the land through which he passed was rich in hides, in fish, in salt, in train-oil, in furs, in pitch, and timber; while it was poor in many other things besides cotton shirts and pewter pots. Sailing up the Dvina to Vologda, he noted that town as a place for future trade; crossed the water-shed of Central Russia to Jaroslav and Moscow; dropped down the river Oka; and fell into the Volga at Nijni, the only town in which trade was being done, until he reached the Caspian Sea. The Volga banks were overrun by Tartar hordes, who took their spoil from every farm, and only spared the towns from fear. In ten weeks his rafts reached Astrakhan, where he saw, to his great surprise and joy, the riches of Persia and Bokhara lying about in the bazaars in heaps; the alum, galls, and spices; the gems and filigrees, the shawls and bands, which he knew would fetch more in the London markets than their weight in gold. By hugging the northern shores of the Caspian Sea, he made the port of Mangishlak, in the Khanate of Khiva, early in autumn; and hiring from the natives a thousand camels, he loaded these patient beasts with his pots and pans, his sheetings and shirtings, and marched by the caravan road over the Tamdi Kuduk to Khiva, and thence, across the range of Sheikh Djeli, and along the skirts of the great desert of Kizil Kum to Bokhara, near the gates of which he encamped on the day before Christmas Eve. There, to his grief, he learned that the caravan road farther east was stopped, in consequence of a war between tribes in the hill country of Turkestan; and after resting in the city of Bokhara for some weeks he gave up his project, and turning his face to the westward, returned to Moscow and London by the roads which he had found.

Three years later he was again in Moscow, chaffering with raftsmen for a voyage to the Caspian Sea. Queen Bess was now on the throne, and Jenkinson bore a letter from his sovereign to the Tsar, suggesting the benefits of trade and intercourse between his people and the Society; and asking for his kingly help in opening up his towns and ports.

Ivan the Terrible was quick to perceive how much his power might be increased by the arts and arms which these strangers could bring him in their ships. Like Peter the Great in his genius for war,

Ivan was only too well aware that, in comparison with the Swedes and Poles, his people were savages; and that his troops, though brave as wolves, and hardy as bears, were still no match for such armies as the Baltic powers could send into the field. The glory of his early triumphs in the east and south had been dimmed by defeats inflicted upon him by his civilised enemies, the Poles; and the conquests of Kazan, Siberia, and Astrakhan, were all but forgotten in the reverses of his later years. He wanted ships, he wanted guns; the best of which, he had heard, could be bought for money in Elizabeth's ports, and brought to the Dvina in English ships. He was too great a savage to read the Queen's letter in the way she wished; he cared no whit for maps, and could not bend his mind to the sale of hemp and pewter pots; but he saw in the Queen's letter, which was addressed to him as Tsar, a recognition of the rank he had assumed, and the offer of a connexion which he hoped to turn into a political alliance of the two powers.

While Ivan was weaving his net of policy, the English rafts were dropping down the Volga, towards Astrakhan, through hordes of Tartar horse. From Astrakhan they coasted the Caspian towards the south, landed at the port of Shabran; and passing over the Georgian Alps, rode on camels through Shemaka and Ardabil, to Kasbin, then a residence of the Persian Shah. To him the Queen had also sent a letter of friendship, and Jenkinson proposed to draw the great lines of Persian traffic by the Caspian and the Volga, to Archangel; connecting

London and Kasbin by a near, a cheap, and an easy road; passing through the countries of a single prince, a natural ally of the Shah and of the Queen, instead of through the territories and waters of the Turk, the Venetian, the Almaigne, and the Dutch. The scheme was bold and new; of vast importance to the Russ, who had then no second outlet to the sea. But the Shah had just made peace with his enemy the Sultan, which compelled him to restore the ancient course of trade between the East and West.

Four years later, William Johnson, also an agent of the Society, was sent from Archangel to Kasbin, with orders to make a good map of the River Volga and the Caspian Sea, and to build an English factory at Astrakhan for the Persian and Chinese trade. The Dvina was also studied and laid down, and the countries dividing her upper waters from the Volga were explored. A track had been worn by the natives from Vologda, one of the antique towns of Moscovy, famous for bells and candles, to Jaroslav on the Volga; and along this track it was possible to transport the bales and boxes of English goods. This line was now laid down for the Persian and Oriental trade to follow, and factories were built in convenient spots along the route; the head-quarters being fixed at Archangel and Astrakhan.

The Tsar sent home by Jenkinson not only a public letter to the Queen, in which he asked her to send him cannon and ships, with men who could sail them; but a secret and verbal message, in which he proposed to make such a treaty of peace and alliance with her, as that they should have the same friends and the same foes; and that if either of the two rulers should have need to quit his states, he might retire with safety and honour into those of the other. To the first, he received no answer, and when Jenkinson returned to Russia on his trade affairs, the Tsar, who thought he had not delivered his message word for word, received him coldly, and ill-used the merchants in his empire; on which Thomas Randolph, a wily and able minister, was sent from London to pacify the tyrant, and protect our countrymen from his rage. But Randolph was treated worse than all; for on his arrival at Moscow, he was not only refused an audience, but placed in such custody that every one saw he was a prisoner. The letters sent to him by the Queen were kept back, and those which he wrote to her were opened and returned. After eight months were passed in these insults, he was called to Vologda, received by the Tsar, and commanded to quit the Russian soil. So much insolence was used, that he was told by one of the boyars if he were not quick in going, they would pitch his baggage out-of-doors.

Yet Randolph, patient and experienced, kept his temper, and when he left the Tsar he had a commercial charter in his trunk, and a special agent of Ivan in his train. This agent, Andrew Gregorivitch, bore a letter to the Queen (in Russ), in which he prayed her to sign a treaty of war and peace against all the world, and to grant him an asylum in her realm in case he should be driven from his own. Andrew found that the Queen could make no treaty of the kind, though she was ready to promise his master an asylum in her states, where he might practise his own religion, and live at his own expense. He then gave ear to an impostor named Eli Bomel, a native of Wesel, whom he found in an English jail. This wretch, who professed to work by magic and the stars, proposed to go with Andrew to Russia and serve the Tsar. The Agent asked for a pardon, and took him out to Moscow, where he soon became master in the tyrant's house. For Bomel made the Tsar believe that the Queen, whom he described as a young and lovely virgin, was in love with him, and could be brought by sorcery to accept an offer of his hand and throne. The Tsar, who was past his prime, and feeble in health and power, never tired of doing honour to the man who promised him an alliance which would raise him above the proudest Emperors and Kings.

Horsey, following Randolph to Russia, saw the end of this wizard. When the Tsar found out that Bomel was deceiving him with lies, and that the Queen would not write to him except on questions of trade, he sent for his favourite, laid him on the rack, drew his legs out of their sockets, flayed him with wire whips, roasted him before a fire, drew him on a sledge through the snow, and pitched him into a dungeon, where he was left to die.

Traders poured into Russia, through the line now opened from the Dvina to the Volga, stores of dyed cotton, copper pots and pans, sheets of lead rolled up for use, and articles in tin and iron of sundry sorts. Thomas Bannister and Geoffrey Ducket reached Jaroslav early in July, and loading a fleet of rafts, dropped down the Volga to Astrakhan; where they stayed six weeks in daily peril of their lives. The Turks, now friends with the Persians, were trying to recover that city, with the low countries of the Volga, from the Christian Russ; and the traders could not put to sea, until the Moslem forces were drawn off. They put into Shabran, where they left their ship, and crossed the mountains on camels to Shemaka, where they stayed for the winter. Not before April, could they venture to take the road. They pushed on to Ardabil, where they began to trade, while Bannister went on to Kasbin, and procured a charter of commerce from the Shah. Only one objection was raised at Kasbin; Bannister wished to send horses through the Shah's dominions into India; but an article which he had inserted in his paper to this effect, was left out by the Persian scribes. The successful trader sickened near Shemaka and died; leaving the command of his adventure to Ducket, who gathered up the goods for which they had exchanged their cloth and hardware, crossed the mountains to Shabran, and put to sea. Storm met them in the teeth; they rolled and tumbled through the waves; and after buffeting the winds for twenty days, they anchored in shallow water, where they were suddenly attacked by a horde of Moslem rievers, and after a gallant fight were overcome by superior strength. The Tartars pulled them from their ship, of which they made a prize, and putting them into their own cutter let them drift to sea. The cargo lost was worth no less than forty thousand pounds:—a quarter of a million in our present coin.

At Astrakhan, which they reached in safety, they made some efforts to recover from the brigands part of what they had lost, and by the general's help some trifles were recovered from the wreck; but this salvage was lost once more in ascending the Volga, on which their boat was crushed by a ridge of ice. Everything on board went down, and the grim old tyrant, Ivan the Terrible, sore about his failing suit for Elizabeth's hand, would render them no help.

Ten years elapsed before the traders sent another caravan across the Georgian Alps, but the road from Archangel to Astrakhan was never closed again; and for many years to come the English public heard far more about the Eastern Steppe than they hear in the present day.

This Eastern Steppe is overrun to-day, as it was overrun in the time of Ducket, by a tameless rabble of Asiatic tribes.

CHAPTER XXX.

Eastern Steppe.

The main attempt to colonise any portion of the Eastern Steppe with Christians, was the planting of a line of Kozak camps in the countries lying between the Volga and the Don—a region in which the soil is less parched, the sand less deep, the herbage less scanty, than elsewhere in these sterile plains. But even in this favoured region the fight for life is so hard and constant, that these Kozak colonists hail with joy the bugles that call them to arm and mount for a distant raid.

A wide and windy plain, sooty in colour, level to the sight, with thin brown moss, and withered weeds; a herd of half-wild horses here and there; a Kalmuk rider dashing through a cloud of dust; a stray camel; a waggon drawn by oxen, ploughing heavily in the mud and marl; a hollow, dark and amber, in which lies a gipsy village; caravans of carts carrying hay and melons; a flock of sheep, watched by a Kozak lad attired in a fur cap, a skin capote, and enormous boots; a windmill on a lonely ridge; a mighty arch of sky overhead, shot with long lines of green and crimson light—such is an evening picture of the Eastern Steppe.

Time out of mind two hostile forces have been flowing from the deserts of Central Asia through this Eastern Steppe towards the fertile districts watered by the Don. These forces are the Turkish and Mongolian tribes. A cloud hangs over the earlier movements of these tribes; but when the invaders come under European ken, they are seen to be divided by differences of type and creed. The Turkish races rank among the handsomest on earth, the Mongolian races rank among the ugliest on earth. The Turkish tribes are children of Mohammed, the Mongolian tribes are children of Buddha. The first are a settled people, living in towns, and tilling the soil; the second, a nomadic people, dwelling in tents, and roving from plain to plain with their flocks and herds.

The Moslem hordes which crossed the Ural River, settled on the Steppe, built cities on the Volga and the Donets, pushed their conquests up to the gates of Kief. The Buddhistic hordes which fought under Batu Khan, destroyed this earlier work; but when they settled on the Steppe, and married Moslem women, many of these heirs of Batu Khan embraced the religion of their wives, and helped the True Believers to erect such cities in their rear as Khiva, Bokhara, Samarcand, and Balkh, which afterwards became the strongholds of their faith. Yet most of the Mongol princes held by their ancient creed, and all the new-comers from their country added to their strength on this Eastern Steppe. These Turks and Mongols, enemies in Asia, kept up their feuds in Europe; and the early Moslem settlers in these plains were sorely pressed by their Buddhistic rulers, until the arrival of Timour Beg restored the Crescent to its old supremacy on the Eastern Steppe.

This feud between Buddha and Mohammed led in these countries to the final triumphs of the Cross.

The plains on which they fought for twenty generations are even now tented and cropped by Asiatic tribes; Kalmuks, Kirghiz, Nogays, Gipsies. The Kalmuks are Buddhists, the Kirghiz and Nogays are Moslem, the Gipsies are simply Gipsies.

The Kalmuks, a pastoral and warlike people, never yet confined in houses, are the true proprietors of the Steppe. But they have given it up; at least in part; for in the reign of Empress Catharine, five hundred thousand wanderers crossed the Ural River, never to come back. The Kirghiz, Turkomans, and Nogays, came in and occupied their lands.

The Kalmuks who remain in the country live in corrals (temporary camps), formed by raising a number of lodges near each other, round the tent of their high-priest. A Kalmuk lodge is a frame of poles set up in the form of a ring, tented at the top, and hung with coarse brown cloth. Inside, the ground is covered with skins and furs, on which the inmates lounge and sleep. Ten, twenty, fifty persons of all ages live under a common roof. A savage is not afraid of crowding; least of all, when he lies down at night. Crowds comfort him and keep him warm. A flock of sheep, a string of camels, and a herd of horses, browse around the corral; for horses, sheep, and camels are the only wealth of tribes who plant no tree, who build no house, who sow no field. Flat in feature, bronze in colour, bony in frame, the Kalmuk is one of the ugliest types of living men, though he is said to produce by mixture with the more flexible and feminine Hindoo the splendid face and figure of the Circassian chief.

The Kalmuk, as a Buddhist, keeping to his ancient Mongol traditions, and worshipping the Dalai-Lama, eats bull beef, but slightly cooked, and drinks mare's milk in his favourite forms of kumis and spirit; the first being milk fermented only, the second milk fermented and distilled. Like all his race, he will steal a cow, a camel, or a horse, from either friend or foe, whenever he finds his chance. He owes no allegiance, he knows no law. Some formal acts of obedience are expected from him; such as paying his taxes, and supplying his tale of men for the ranks; but these payments and supplies are nominal only, save in districts where the rover has settled down under Kozak rule.

These wild men come and go as they list, roving with their sheep and camels from the wall of China to the countries watered by the Don. They come in hordes, and go in armies. In the reign of Michael Romanoff fifty thousand Kalmuks poured along the Eastern Steppe; and these unwelcome guests were afterwards strengthened by a second horde of ten thousand tents. These Kalmuks treated with Peter the Great as an independent power, and for several generations they paid no tribute to the Crown, except by furnishing cavalry in time of war. Another horde of ten thousand tents arrived. Their prince, Ubasha, led an army of thirty thousand horsemen towards the Danube against the Turks; whom they hated as only Asiatics hate hereditary foes. Yet, on the Empress Catharine trying to place the hordes under rule and law, the same Ubasha led his tribes —five hundred thousand souls, with countless herds of cattle, camels, and horses—back from the Eastern Steppe, across the Ural river into Asia; stripping whole provinces of their wealth, producing famine in the towns, and robbing the empire of her most powerful arm. Hurt in his pride, by some light word from the imperial lips, the Prince proposed to carry off all his people; leaving not a soul behind; but fifteen thousand tents were left, because the winter came down late, and the Volga ice was thin. The children of these laggers are the men you meet on the plains, surprise at their religious rites, and sup with in their homely tents. Steps have been often taken to reclaim and fix these rovers, but with little or no effect. Some families have joined the Kozaks, come under law, and even embraced the Cross; but the vast majority cling to their wild life, their Asiatic dress, and their Buddhistic creed.

The upper classes are called White (literally white bones), the lower classes Black, just as in Asiatic fashion the Russian nobles are called White, while the peasants are called Black.

The Kirghiz are of Turkish origin, and speak the Uzbek idiom of their race. Divided into three branches, called the Great Horde, the Middle Horde, and the Little Horde, they roam over, if they do not own, the steppes and deserts lying between the Volga and Lake Balkash. Much of this tract is sandy waste, with dots of herbage here and there, and most of it lies beyond the Russian lines. Within these lines some order may be kept; beyond them, in what is called the Independent Steppe, the Kirghiz devilry finds an open field. These children of the desert plunder friend and foe, not only lifting cattle, and robbing caravans, but stealing men and women to sell as slaves. All through these deserts, from Fort Aralsk to Daman-i-Koh, the slave-trade is in vogue; the Kirghiz bandits keeping the markets of Khiva and Bokhara well supplied with boys and girls for sale. Nor is the traffic likely to decline, until the flag of some civilised people floats from the Tower of Timour Beg. Fired by hereditary hate, these Kirghiz bandits look on every man of Mongolian birth and Buddhistic faith as lawful spoil. They follow him to his pastures, plunder his tent, drive off his herds, and sell him as a slave. But when this lawful prey escapes their hands they raid and rob on more friendly soil; and many of the captives whom they carry to Khiva and Bokhara come from the Persian valleys of Atrek and Meshid. Girls from these valleys fetch a higher price, and Persia has not strength enough to protect her children from their raids.

When Ubasha fled from the Volga with his Kalmuk hosts, these Kirghiz had a year of sweet revenge. They lay in wait for their retiring foes; they broke upon their camps by night; they stole their horses; they devoured their food; they carried off their women. Hanging on the flank and rear of this moving mass, they cut off stragglers, stopped communications, hid the wells; inflicting far more miseries on the Kalmuks than these rovers suffered from all the generals sent against them by the Crown.

These Kalmuks gone, the Kirghiz crossed the borders, and appeared on the Volga, where they have been well received. Their Khan is rich and powerful; and in coming in contact with Europe, he has learned to value science; but the attempts which have been made to settle some portions of his tribe at Ryn Peski have met with no success. The Emperor has built a house for the Khan, but the Khan himself, preferring to live out of doors, has pitched his tent on the lawn! A Bedouin of the Desert is not more untameable than a Kirghiz of the Steppe.

The Nogays are Mongolians of a separate horde. Coming into the country with Jani Beg they spread themselves through the southern plains, took wives of the people, and embraced the Mussulman faith. At first they were a nomadic soldiery, living in camps; and even after the war had died out, they kept to their waggons, and roamed through the country as the seasons came and went. "We live on wheels," they used to say: "One man has a house on the ground, another man has a house on wheels. It is the will of God." Yet, in the course of five hundred years, these Nogays have in some measure changed their habits of life, though they have not changed their creed. Many of them are settlers on the land, which they farm in a rough style; growing millet, grapes, and melons, for their daily food. Being strict Mohammedans, they drink no wine, and marry two or three wives a-piece. All wives are bought with money; and divorce, though easy to obtain, is seldom tried. The men are proud of their descent and their religion, and the Crown allows their cadis and mollahs to settle most of their disputes. They pay a tax, but they are not enrolled for war.

These Mongolians occupy the Russian steppe between the Molochnaya River and the Sea of Azof.

The Gipsies, here called Tsiganie, live a nomadic life in the Eastern Steppe, as in other countries, sleeping in wretched tents of coarse brown cloth, and grovelling like dogs and swine in the mire. They own a few carts, and ponies to match the carts, in which they carry their wives and little folk from fair to fair, stealing poultry, telling fortunes, shoeing horses, and existing only from hand to mouth. They will not labour—they will not learn. Some Gipsies show a talent for music, and many of their girls have a beauty of person which is highly prized. A few become public singers; and a splendid specimen of her race may marry —like the present Princess Sergie Galitzin of Moscow—into the highest rank; but as a race they live apart, in true Asiatic style; reiving and prowling on their neighbours' farms, begging at one house, thieving at the next; a class of outlaws; objects of fear to many, and of disgust to all. In summer they lodge on the grass, in winter they burrow in the ground; taking no more thought of the heat and dew than of the frost and snow. In colour they are almost bronze, with big fierce eyes and famished looks, as though they were the embodied life of the dirt in which they wallow by day and dream by night. Some efforts have been made by Government to civilise these mysterious tribes, but hitherto without results; and the marauders are only to be kept in check on the Eastern Steppe by occasional onsets of Kozak horse.

CHAPTER XXXI.

Don Kozaks.

SINCE the flight of their countrymen under Ubasha, the Kalmuks have been closely pressed by their Moslem foes.

Their chief tormentors came from the Caucasus; from the hills of which countries, Nogays and Turkomans, eternal enemies of their race and faith, descended on their pasture lands, drove out their sheep and camels, broke up their corrals, and insulted their religious rites. No government could prevent these raids, except by following the raiders home. But then, these Nogays and Turkomans were independent tribes; their homes were built on the heights beyond the Russian lines; and the necessities under which Russia lay—first, to protect her own plains from insult; next, to preserve the peace between these Buddhists and Moslems, gave her a better excuse for occupying the hill-countries in her front, than the sympathy felt in high quarters for the Georgian Church. Pressed by these enemies, some of the Kalmuks have appealed to the crown for help, and have even quitted their camps, and sought protection within the Kozak lines.

The Kozak camps along the outer and inner frontiers,—the Ural line and the Volga line—are peopled by a mixed race of Malo-Russians, Kalmuks, and Kirghiz; but the element that fuses and connects these rival forces comes from the old free Ukraine, and is thoroughly Slavonic in creed and race.

A Kozak of the Volga and the Don is not a Russian of Moscow, but of Novgorod and Kief; a man who, for hundreds of years, has held his own. His horse is always saddled; his lance is always sharp. By day and night his face is towards the enemy; his camp is in a state of siege. Compared with a Russian of Moscow, the Kozak is a jovial fellow, heady and ready, prompt in remark, and keen in jest; his mouth full of song, his head full of romance, and his heart full of love.

On the Ural river, the Kozak has a little less of the Kalmuk, a little more of the Kirghiz, in his veins; but the Ukraine blood is dominant in both. It would be impossible for the Kalmuk and Kirghiz to live in peace, if these followers of the Grand Lama and the Arabian Prophet were not held in check by the Kozak camps.

First at St. Romanof, afterwards at Cemikarakorskoe, and other camps on the Don, I find the Kozaks in these camps; eat and drink with them, join in their festivals, watch their dances, hear their national songs, and observe them fight their fights. An aged story-teller comes into my room at St. Romanof, to spin long yarns about Kozak daring and adventure in the Caucasian wars. I notice as a peculiarity of these gallant recitals, that the old warrior's stories turn on practices and stratagems, never on open and manly fights; the tricks by which a picket was misled, a village captured, a caravan cut off, a heap of booty won. As the old man speaks of a farm-yard entered, of a herd of cows surprised, his face will gleam with a sudden joy; and then the younkers listening to his tale will clap their hands and stamp their feet, impatient to mount their stallions and ride away. When he tells of harems forced and mosques profaned, the Kalmuks who are present colour and pant with Asiatic glee.

These Kozaks live in villages, composed of houses and gardens built in a kind of maze; the houses thatched with straw, the walls painted yellow; and a ring-fence running round the cluster of habitations, with an opening only at two or three points. The ins and outs are difficult; the passages guarded by savage dogs; the whole camp being a pen for the cattle as well as a fortress for the men. A church, of no great size and splendour, springs from the highest mound in the hamlet; for these Kozaks of the Eastern Steppe, are nearly all attached to the Ancient Slavonic Rite. A flock of sheep is baa-ing on the Steppe, a train of carts and oxen moving on the road. A fowler crushes through the herbage with his gun. On every side we see some evidence of life; and if the plain is still dark and bare, the Kozak love of 'garden, fence, and colour, lends a charm to the Southern country never to be seen in the North.

A thousand souls are camped at St. Romanof, in a rude hamlet, with the usual paint and fence. Each house stands by itself, with its own yard and garden, vines, and melon-beds, guarded by a savage dog. The type is Malo-Russ, the complexion yellow and Tartar-like; the teeth are very fine, the eyes are burning with hidden fire. Men and boys all ride, and every child appears to possess a horse. Yet half the men are nursing babies, while the women are doing the heavier kinds of work. A superstition of the Steppe accounts for the fact of half these men carrying infants in their arms, the naked brats pressed closely beneath their coats. They think that unless a father nurses his first-born son, his wife will die of the second child; and as a woman costs so many cows and horses, it is a serious thing—apart from his affections—for a man on the Eastern Steppe to lose his wife.

No smoking is allowed in a Kozak camp, for dread of fire; though my host at Cemikarakorskoe smokes himself, and invites his guests to smoke. Outside the fence, the women are frying melons and making wine; a strong and curious liquor, thick as treacle, with a finer taste. It is an ancient custom —lost—except on the Don. A plain church, with a lofty belfry, adorns the camp; but a majority of the Kozaks being Old Believers, the camp may be said to absent itself from mass. These rough fellows, ready as they seem for raiding and thieving, are just now overwhelmed with sorrow on account of their church affairs!

Their bishop, Father Plato, has been seized in his house at Novo Cherkask, and sent up the Don to Kremenskoe, a convent near Kalatch. A very old man, he has now been two years a prisoner in that convent; and no one in the camp can learn the nature of his offence. The Kozaks bear his trouble with saddened hearts and flashing eyes; for these colonists look on the board of Black clergy sitting in St. Isaac's Square, not only as a conclave going beyond its functions, but as the Chert, the Black One, the incarnate Evil Spirit.

Cemikarakorskoe is a chief camp or town on the Lower Don. "How many souls have you in camp?" I ask my host, as we stroll about. "We do not know; our folk don't relish counting; but we have always five hundred saddles ready in the stalls." The men look wild; but they are gradually taming down. Fine herds of cattle dot the plains beyond their fence, and some of the families sow fields of corn and maize. They grow abundance of purple grapes, from which they press a strong and sparkling wine. My host puts on his table a vintage as good as Asti; and some folk say the vineyards of the Don are finer than those of the Garonne and the Marne!

These Kozaks have soil enough to grow their food, and fill the markets with their surplus. No division of land has taken place for thirty-two years. A plain extends in front, as far as the eye can reach; it is a common property, and every man can take what he likes. The poorest fellows have thirty acres a-piece. In their home affairs, these Colonists are still a state within the State. Their hetman has been abolished; their Grand Ataman is the Crown Prince; but his work is wholly nominal; and they elect their own atamans and judges for a limited term. Every one is eligible for the office of local ataman; a Colonel of the camp, who commands the village in peace and war; but he must not leave his quarters for the whole of his three years. An officer is sent from St. Petersburg to drill and command the troops. Every one is eligible as judge; an officer who tries all cases under forty rubles of account; and like an ataman, the judge may not quit his village, even in time of war.

A great reform is taking place among these camps. All officers above the rank of ataman and judge are now appointed by the crown, as such men are in every branch of the public force. An Ataman-general resides with an effective staff at Novo Cherkask, a town lying back from the Don, in a position to guard against surprise; a town with streets and houses, and with thoroughfares lit by lamps instead of being watched by savage dogs. But Novo Cherkask is a Russian city, not a Kozak camp; the Ataman-general is a Russian soldier, not a Kozak chief; and the object kept in view at Novo Cherkask is that of safely and steadily bringing these old military colonists on the Eastern Steppe under the action of imperial law.

But such a change must be a work of time. General Potapoff, the last ruler in Novo Cherkask, a man of high talents, fell to his work so fast that a revolt seemed likely to occur along the whole line of the Don. On proof that he was not the man for such a post, this general was promoted to Vilna, as commander-in-chief in the Fourth Military

District; while General Chertkoff, a man of conservative views, was sent down from St. Petersburg to soothe the camps and keep things quiet in the Steppe. The Emperor made a little joke on his officers' names:—"After the Flood, the Devil;" Potop meaning deluge, and Chert the Evil One; and when his brave Kozaks had laughed at the jest, everything fell back for a time into the ancient ruts.

Of course, in a Free Russia all men must be put on an equal footing before the law, and Kozak privilege must go the way that every other privilege is going. Yet where is the class of men that willingly gives up a special right?

A Kozak is a being slow to change; and a prince who has to keep his eye fixed day and night on these Eastern steppes, and on the cities lying beyond them, Khiva and Bokhara, out of which have come from age to age those rolling swarms of savage tribes, can hardly be expected, even in the cause of uniform law, to break his lines of defence, and drive his faithful pickets into open revolt against his rule.

CHAPTER XXXII.

Under Arms.

An army is in every state, whether bond or free, a thing of privilege and tradition; and in giving a new spirit to his government, it is essential that the Emperor should bring his army into some closer relation to the country he is making free.

The first thing is to raise the profession of arms to a higher grade, by giving to every soldier in the ranks the old privilege of a prince and boyar —his immunity from blows and stripes. A soldier cannot now be flogged. Before the present reign, the army was in theory an open school of merit, and occasionally a man like General Skobeleff, rose from the rank of peasant to the highest posts. But Skobeleff was a man of genius; a good writer, as well as a splendid soldier; and his nomination as commander of St. Petersburg took no one by surprise. Such cases of advancement are extremely rare; rare as in the Austrian service, and in our own. But the reforms now introduced into the army are making this opening for talent wide enough to give every one a chance. The soldiers are better taught, better clothed, and better lodged. In distant provinces, they are not yet equal to the show-troops seen on a summer day at Tsarskoe Seloe; but they are lodged and treated, even in these far-off stations, with a care to which aforetime they were never used. Every man has a pair of strong boots, a good over-coat, a bashlik for his head. His rations are much improved; good beef is weighed to him; and he is not compelled to fast. The brutal punishment of Running the Ranks has been put down.

A man who served in the army, just before the Crimean War broke out, put the difference between the old system and the new in a luminous way.

"God bless the Emperor," he said; "he gave me life, and all that I can give him in return is his."

"You were a prisoner, then?"

"I was a soldier, young and hot. Some Kozak blood was in my veins; unlike the serfs, I could not bear a blow; and broke my duty as a soldier to escape an act of shame."

"For what were you degraded?"

"Well! I was a fool. A fool? I was in love; and staked my liberty for a pretty girl. I kissed her, and was lost."

"That is what the greatest conquerors have done. You lost yourself for a rosy lip?"

"Well—yes; and—no," said Michael. "You see I was a youngster then. A man is not a greybeard when he counts his nineteen summers; and a pair of bright eyes, backed by a saucy tongue, is more than a lad of spirit can pass without a singe. Katinka's eyes were bright as her words were arch. You see, in those days we were all young troops on the road;

going down from Yaroslav, into the south, to fight for the Holy Cross and the Golden Keys. The Frank and Turk were coming up into our towns, to mock our religion and to steal our wives; and after a great festa in the Church, when the golden icon was brought round the ranks, and every man kissed it in his turn, we marched out of Yaroslav, with rolling drums, and pious hymns, and blessings on our arms. The town soon dropped behind us, and with the steppe in front, we turned back more than once to look at the shining domes and towers, which few of us could hope to see again. For three days we kept well on; the fourth day, some of our lads were missing; for the roads were heavy, the wells were almost dry, and the regiment was badly shod. Many were sick; but some were feigning; and the punishment for shamming is the rod. Our Colonel, a tall, gaunt fellow, stiff as a pike and tight as a cord, whom no fatigue could touch, began to flog the stragglers; and as every man in the ranks had to take his turn in whipping his fellows, the temper of the whole regiment became morose and savage. In those old times—some eighteen years ago—we had a rough and ready sort of punishment, called running the ranks."

"Running the ranks?"

"It is done so:—if a lad has either fallen asleep on his post, or vexed his officer, or stolen his comrade's pipe, or failed to answer at the roll, he is called to the parade-ground of his company, told to give up his gun, and strip himself naked to the waist. A soldier grounds the musket, to which the culprit's two hands are now tied fast near the muzzle; the bayonet is then fixed, and the butt-end lifted from the ground, so as to bring the point of the bayonet close to the culprit's heart. The company is then drawn up in two long lines, in open order; and into every man's hand is given a rod newly cut and steeped for a night in water to make it hard. The offender is led between these lines; led by the butt-end of his gun, the slightest motion of which he must obey, on pain of being pricked to death; and the troops lay on his naked back, with a will or not, as their mood may chance to be. The pain is always great; and the sufferer dares not shrink before the rod, as in doing so he would fall on the bayonet point. But the shame of running the ranks was greater than the pain. Some fellows learned to bear it; but these were men who had lost all sense of shame. For my own part, I think it was worse than death and hell."

"You have not borne it?"

"Never! I will tell you. We had marched about a thousand versts towards the south. Our companies were greatly thinned; for every second man who had left Yaroslav with beating heart and singing his joyous psalm, was left behind us, either in the sickward or on the steppe—most of them on the steppe. Many of the men had run away; some because they did not want to fight; and others because they had vexed their officers by petty faults. We had a fortnight yet to march before reaching those lines of Perekop, where the Tartars used to fight us; and our stiff colonel cried out daily down our squads, that if we skulked on the march the Turks would be in Moscow, not the Russians at Stamboul."

"Yes!"

"We had a fortnight yet to march; but the men were so spent and sore, that we halted in a roadside village three days to mend our shoes and recruit our strength. That halt unmade me. What with her laughing eyes and her merry tricks, the girl who served out whisky and halibut to our company won my heart. Her father kept the inn and posting-house of the village; he had to find us quarters, and supply us with meat and drink. The girl was about the sheds in which we lay from early morning until late at night. I don't say she cared for me, though I was thought a handsome lad; but she was like a wild kitten, and would purr and play about you till your blood was all on fire; and into the stable or the straw-shed, screaming with laughter and daring you to chase and capture her—with a kiss, of course. It was rare good sport; but some of the men, too broken to engage in making love, were jealous of the fun, and said it would end in trouble. Well, when the drum tapped for our companies to fall-in, my cloak was missing, and I began to hunt through the shed in which we had slept the last three nights. The cloak could not be found. While running up and down, upsetting stools and scattering sheaves of straw, I caught Katinka's laughing face at the window of the shed, and at the very same instant heard the word of command to march. I had no intention to quit the ranks; but I wanted my cloak, the loss of which would have been visited upon me by the anger of my captain and by the wintry frosts. I ran after Katinka, who darted round the sheds, with the cloak on her arm, crowing with delight as she slipped through the stakes and past the corners, until she bounded into the straw-yard, panting and spent. To get the cloak from her was the work of a second; but to smother her red mouth with kisses was a task which must have taken me some time; for just as I was getting free from her, two men of my company came up and took me prisoner. Grey-beards of twenty-five, who had seen what they call the world, these fellows cared no more for a pretty girl than for a holy saint. They told the colonel lies; they said I meant to straggle and desert; and the officers sentenced me to run the ranks."

·"You escaped the shame?"

"By taking my chance of death. The colonel stood before me, bolt upright, his hand upon the shoulder of his horse. Too well I knew how to merit death in a time of war; and striding up to him, by a rapid motion, ere any one could pull me back, I struck that officer with my open palm across his cheek. A minute later I was pinioned, thrown into a cart, and placed under a double guard. At Perekop I was brought before commissioners and condemned to die; but the Franks were now coming up the Bosphorus in ships, and the Prince commanding in the Crimea, being anxious to make the war popular, was in a tender mood; and finding that my record in the regiment was good, he changed my sentence of death into one of imprisonment in a fortress during life. My comrades thought I should be pardoned in a few weeks and placed in some other company for service; but my crime was too black to be forgiven in that iron reign."

"Iron reign?"

"The reign of Nicolas was the iron reign. I was sent to a fortress, where I lay, a prisoner, until Nicolas went to heaven."

"You lived two years in jail?"

"Lived! No; you do not live in jail; you die. But when the saints are cross you take a very long time to die."

"You wished to die?"

"Well, no; you only wish to sleep, to forget your pain, to escape from the watcher's eyes. When the rings are soldered round your ankles, and the cuffs are fastened round your wrists, you feel that you have ceased to be a man. Cold, passive, cruel in your temper, you are now a savage beast, without the savage freedom of the wolf and bear. Your legs swell out, and your bones grow gritty, and like to snap."

"Which are the worse to bear, the leg-rings or the cuffs?"

"The cuffs. When they are taken off, a man goes all but mad. He clasps and claps his hands for joy; he can lift his palms in prayer; besides being able to chase the spiders and kill the fleas. Worst of all to the prisoner are the eyelets in his door, through which the sentinel watches him from dawn to dusk. Though lonely, he is never alone. Do what he may, the passionless holes are open, and a freezing glance may be fixed upon him. In his sleeping, and in his waking hour, those eyes are on him, and he gladly waits for darkness to come down, that he may feel secure from that maddening watch. Sometimes a man goes boldly to the door, spits through the holes, yells like a wild beast, and forces the sentinel to retire in shame."

"You gained your freedom in the general amnesty?"

"Yes; when the young prince came to his throne, he opened our prison-doors and set us free. Were you ever a prisoner? No! Then you can never know what it is to be free. You walk out of darkness into light; you wake out of misery into joy. The air you breathe makes you strong like a draught of wine. You feel that you belong to God."

Under Nicolas the soldiers were so dressed and drilled that they were always falling sick. A third of the army was in hospital the whole year round, and little more than half the men could ever be returned as fit to march. Being badly clothed and poorly fed, they flew to drink. They died in heaps, and rather like sheep than men.

The case is different now; for the soldier is better clothed and fed than persons of his class in ordinary life. The men are allowed to stand and walk in their natural way; and having more bread to eat, they show less craving after drink. A school is opened in every barrack, and pressure is put on the men to make them learn. Many of the soldiers can read, and some can write. Gazettes and papers are taken in; libraries are being formed; and the Russian army promises to become as bright as that of Germany or France. The change is great; and every one finds the root of this reform in that abolition of the Tartar stick which comes, like other great reforms, from the Crimean War.

CHAPTER XXXIII.

Alexander.

THE Crimean War restored the people to their national life. "Sevastopol!" said a general officer to me just now, "Sevastopol perished, that our country might be free." The Tartar kingdom, founded by Ivan the Terrible, reformed by Peter the Great, existed in the spirit, even where it clothed itself in western names and forms, until the Allies landed from their transports. Routed on the Alma, beaten at Balaklava, that kingdom made her final effort on the heights of Inkermann; hurling, in Tartar force and fashion, her last "great horde" across that Baidar valley, in the rocks and caves of which a remnant of the tribes of Batu Khan and Timour Beg still lingers; fighting in mist and fog, on wooded slope and stony ridge, her gallant and despairing fight. What followed Inkermann was detail only. Met and foiled that wintry day, she reeled and bled to death. A grave was made for her, as one may say, not far from the spot on which she fought and fell. Before the landing-place, in Sevastopol, sprang the walls and frowned the guns of an imperial fort; the strongest pile in Russia, perhaps in Europe; rising tier on tier, and armed with two hundred and sixty guns; a fort in the fire of which no ship then floating on the sea could live. It bore the builder's name; the name of Nicolas, Autocrat of all the Russians; a colossal sovereign, who for thirty years had awed and stifled men like Genghis Khan. That fort became a ruin. The guns were torn to rag, the walls were shivered into dust. No stone was left in its place to tell the tale of its former pride; and it is even now an easier task to trace the outlines of Khersones, dead for five hundred years, than to restore, from what remains of them, the features of that proud, imperial fort. The prince, the fortress, and the kingdom, fell; their work on earth accomplished to the final act. This ruin is their grave.

Asiatic Russia passed away, and European Russia struggled into life.

Holding under the "Great Cham," the Duke of Moscow was in ancient times a dependent prince, like the Hospodar of Valachia, like the Pasha of Egypt, in modern days. Doing homage, paying tribute, to his Tartar lord, the Duke ruled in his place, coined money in his name, adopted his dress and habits, fought his battles, and took into pay his officers and troops. Cities which the Tartar could not reach his vassal crushed.

The Tartar system was a village system, as it is with every pastoral and predatory race, a village for the followers, and a camp or residence for the prince. The Russian system was a mixed system, as it was in Germany and France; a village for the husbandman, a town for the boyar, merchant, and professional man. The old Russian towns were rich and free; ruled by codes of law, by popular assemblies, and by elected dukes. Novgorod, Moscow, Pskoff, Vladimir, Nijni, were models of a hundred prosperous towns; but when the Duke of Moscow wrested his independence from the Khan, in the seventeenth century, he took up the Tartar policy of weakening the free cities, and centreing all authority in his camp. That camp was Moscow, which Ivan put under martial law, and governed, in Asiatic fashion, by the stick. The court became a Tartar court. The dress and manners of Bakchi Serai were imitated in the Kremlin; women were put into harems; the Tartar distinction of white and black (noble and ignoble) was established. From the time when the Grand Dukes became Tsars they were called White, the peasants Black; and the poor of every class, whether they lived in towns or villages, were styled, in contempt, as their Moslem masters had always styled them, Christians—bearers of the Cross—a name which descended to the serfs, and clung to them so long as a serf existed on Russian soil.

In leaving Moscow, Peter the Great was only acting like the Crim Tartar who had changed his camp from Eski-Crim to Bakchi Serai. The camp was his country, and where he rested for a season was his camp. In Old Russia, as in Germany and France, authority was historical; in Crim-Tartary, as in Turkey and Bokhara, it was personal. Ivan the Terrible introduced, and Peter the Great extended, the personal system. In her better days, Russia had a noble class as well as a citizen class and a peasant class; but these signs of a glorious past were gradually put away. "No man is noble in my empire, unless I make him so," said Peter. "No man is noble in my empire, except when I speak to him, and only while I speak to him," said Paul. The governors of provinces became Pashas, with the right of living on the districts they were sent to rule; that is to say, of taking from the people meat, drink, house, dogs, horses, women, at their sovereign will.

Though softened from time to time, here by fine phrases, there by mystic patriotism, this Tartar system lived into the present reign. Under this system, the Prince was everything, the People nothing; the Army a horde, the Nobility an official mob, the Church a department of police, the Commons a herd of slaves.

Nicolas prized that system, and being a man of powerful frame and daring mind, he carried it forward to a point from which it had been falling back since the reign of Peter the Great. Unlike Peter, Nicolas saw no use in Western science and Western arts. He hated railways, he abhorred the press. He liked his court to be a camp; to see his students in uniform, to turn education into drill. He was the State, the Church, the Army, all in one. Desiring to shut up his empire, as the Khans of Khiva and Bokhara close their states, he drew a cordon round his frontier, over which it was nearly as difficult for a stranger to enter as for a subject to escape; and while he occupied the throne his country was almost as much a mystery to mankind as the realm of Prester John. With mystery came distrust, for the unknown is always feared; and Europe lay in front of this Tartar prince, exactly as in former ages Moscow lay before Timour Beg. A system such as Nicolas loved, could not exist in presence of free and powerful states; and Europe had to march upon the armies of Nicolas, even as Ivan the Terrible had to march upon the troops of Yediguer Khan.

The system was Mongolian, not Slavonic; and the mighty sovereign who upheld it, and perished with it, will be regarded in future ages as the prince who was at once the last Asiatic Emperor and the last European Khan.

When Alexander the Second came to his sceptre, what was his estate? His empire was a wreck. The Allies were upon his soil; his ports were closed; his ships were sunk; his armies were held at bay. Looking from the Neva to the Thames, he could not see one friend on whom in his trouble he could call for help. The system was perfect; the isolation was complete. But why had that system, reared at such a price, collapsed so thoroughly at the point where it seemed to be most strong?

His armies counted a million men. Why were these hosts unable to protect their soil? They were at home; they knew the country; they were used to its windy plains, its summer heats and its wintry snows. They were fighting, too, for everything that men hold dear on earth. When Alexander compared his million men against the forces of his rivals, actually in the field, his wonder grew into amazement. These soldiers of his foes were weak in number, far from home, and fighting only for pride and pay. How were such armies able to maintain themselves on Russian ground?

Before the Emperor Nicolas died, he read the truth; read it in the light of his burning towns, his wasting armies, and his fruitless cannonades. He found that he and his million troops were matched against a hundred millions of eager and adventurous foes. Free nations were all against him; and the serf nation which he ruled so sternly was not for him. Russia was not with him. Here he was weak, with an incurable fret and sore. The serfs, the Old Believers, and the sectaries of every name, were all against him; looking on his system as a foreign, not to say, an abominable thing; and praying night and day that the hour of their deliverance from his rule might quickly come. No people stood behind the soldiery in his war against the Western Powers.

In spite of genius, valour, enterprise, success, an army fighting for itself, unwarmed by popular applause, is sure in the end to fail. The discovery that he and his troops were fighting against the world of free thought and liberal science killed him. When the blow was dealt, and his pride was gone, Nicolas is said to have confided to his son Alexander the causes of his failure, as he had come to see them, and to have urged the prince to pursue another and more liberal course. Who can say whether this is true or not, for who can know the secrets of that dying bed?

Yet every man can see that the new sovereign acted as if some such warning had been given. ♦ He began his reign with acts of mercy. Hundreds of prison-doors were opened, thousands of exiles were released from bonds. An honourable peace was made with the Western Powers, and the dream of marching on Stamboul was brushed aside. An Empire of seventy millions was found big enough to hold her own. Alexander proved that he had none of the Tartar's lust of territory, by giving up part of Bessarabia for the sake of peace.

Secured on his frontiers, Alexander turned his eyes on the people and the provinces committed to his care. A vast majority of his countrymen were serfs. Not one in ten could read; not one in fifty could sign his name. Great numbers of his people stood aloof from the Official Church. The serfs were much oppressed by the nobles; the Old Believers were bitterly persecuted by the monks; yet these two classes were the bone and sinew of the land. If strength was sought beyond the army and the official classes, where could he find it, save among these serfs in the country, these Old Believers in the towns? In no other places. How could such populations, suffering as they were from physical bondage and religious hate, be reconciled to the Empire, added to the national force?

Studying the men over whom he was called to rule, the Emperor went down among his people; living on their river banks and in their rural communes; passing from the Arctic to the Caspian Sea, from the Vistula to the Ural mines; kneeling with them at Solovetsk and Troitsa; parleying with them on the roadside and by the inland lake; observing them in the forest and in the mine; until he felt that he had seen more of the Russian soil, knew more of the Russian people, than any of the ministers about his court.

In the light of knowledge thus carefully acquired, he opened the great question of the Serfs; and feeling strong in his minute acquaintance with his country, had the happy courage to insist on his principle of "Liberty with Land," against the views of his councils and committees in favour of "Liberty without Land."

Before that act was carried out in every part, he began his great reform in the Army. He put down flogging, beating, and striking in the ranks. He opened schools in the camp; cleared the avenues of promotion; and raised the soldier's condition on the moral, not less than on the material side.

The Universities were then reformed in a pacific sense. Swords were put down, uniforms laid aside, and corporate privileges withdrawn. Education was divorced from its connexion with the camp. Lay professors occupied the chairs, and the young men attending lectures stood on the same level with their fellows, subject to the same magistrate, amenable to the common code. The schools became free, and students ceased to be feared as "servants of the Tsar."

This change was followed by that immense reform in the administration of Justice which transferred the trial of offenders from the police office to the courts of law; replacing an always arbitrary and often corrupted official by an impartial jury, acting in union with an educated judge.

At the same period he opened those local parliaments, the District Assemblies and the Provincial Assemblies, which are training men to think and speak, to listen and decide—to believe in argument, to respect opposing views, and exercise the virtues required in public life.

In the wake of these reforms came the still more delicate question of Church reform; including the relations of the Black clergy to the White; of the Orthodox clergy, whether Black or White, to the Old Believers; of the Holy Governing Synod to Dissenters; as also the influence which the Church should exercise over secular education, and the supremacy of the canon law over the civil law.

Each of these great reforms would seem, in a country like Russia, to require a lifetime; yet, under this daring and beneficent ruler, they are all proceeding side by side. Opposed by the three most powerful parties in the empire,—the Black clergy, who feel that power is slipping from their hands,—the old military chiefs, who think their soldiers should be kept in order by the stick,—the thriftless nobles, who prefer Homberg and Paris to a dull life on their estates—the Emperor not the less keeps steadily working out his ends. What wonder that he is adored by peasants, burghers, and parish priests, by all who wish to live in peace, to till their fields, to mind their shops, and to say their prayers!

A Free Russia is a Pacific Russia. By his genius and his occupation, a Russian is less inclined to war than either a Briton or a Gaul, and as the right of voting on public questions comes to be his habit, his voice will be more and more cast for the policy that gives him peace. In one direction only, he looks with dread; across that opening of the Eastern Steppe through which he has seen so many hordes of his enemies swarm into his towns and fields. Through that opening, he has pushed—is now pushing—and will push his way, until Khiva and Bokhara fall into his power, as Tashkend and Kokan have fallen into his power.

Why should we English regret his march, repine at his success? Is he not fighting for all the world, a battle of law, of order, and of civilisation? Would not Russia at Bokhara mean the English at Bokhara also? Would not roads be made, and stations built, and passes guarded, through the Steppe for traders and travellers of every race? Could any other people undertake this task? Why then should we cry down the Moscovite? Even in our selfish interests, it would be well for us to have a civilised neighbour on our frontier rather than a savage tribe; a neighbour bound by law and courtesy instead of a savage Khan who murders our envoy and rejects our trade!

Russia requires a hundred years of peace; but she will not find that peace until she has closed the passage of her Eastern Steppe by planting the banner of St. George on the tower of Timour Beg.

Meantime, the reforming Emperor holds his course; a lonely man, much crossed by care, much tried by family afflictions, much enduring in his public life.

One dark December day, near dusk, two Englishmen hail a boat on the Neva brink, and push out rapidly through the bars of ice towards that grim fortress of St. Peter and St. Paul, in which lie buried under marble slab and golden cross, the emperors and empresses (with one exception,) since the reign of Peter the Great. As they are pushing onward, they observe the watermen drop their oars and doff their caps; and looking round, they see the imperial barge, propelled by twenty rowers, athwart their stern. The Emperor sits in that barge alone; an officer is standing by his side; and the helmsman directs the rowers how to pull. Saluting as he glides past their boat, the Emperor jumps to land, and muffling his loose grey cloak about his neck, steps hastily along the planks, and up the roadway leading to the church. No one goes with him. The six or eight idlers whom he meets on the road just touch their hats, and stand aside to let him pass. Trying the front door of that sombre church, he finds it locked; and striding off quickly to a second door, he sees a man in plain clothes, and beckons to him. The door is quickly opened, and the Lord of seventy millions walks into the church that is to be his final home. The English visitors are near. "Wait for an instant," says the man in plain clothes; "the Emperor is within;" but adds, "You can step into the porch; his Majesty will not keep you long." The porch is parted from the church by glass doors only; and the English visitors look down upon the scene within. Long aisles and columns stretch and rise before them. Flags and trophies, won in a hundred battles, fought against the Swede and Frank, the Perse and Turk, adorn the walls: and here and there a silver lamp burns fitfully in front of a pictured saint. Between the columns stand, in white sepulchral rows, the imperial tombs; a weird and ghastly vista, gleaming in that red and sombre light.

Alone, his cap drawn tightly on his brow, and muffled in his loose grey coat, the Emperor passes from slab to slab; now pausing for an instant, as if conning an inscription on the stone; now crossing the nave absorbed and bent; here hidden for a moment in the gloom; there moving furtively along the aisle. The dead are all around him; Peter, Catharine, Paul; fierce warriors, tender women, innocent babes; and overhead the dust and glory of a hundred wars. What brings him hither, in this wintry dusk? The weight of life? The love of death? He stops, unbonnets, kneels; at the foot of his mother's tomb! Once more he pauses, kneels;

kneels a long time, as if in prayer; then, rising, kisses the golden cross. That slab is the tomb of his eldest son!

A moment later he is gone.

THE END.

www.ingramcontent.com/pod-product-compliance
Lightning Source LLC
Chambersburg PA
CBHW031938230426
43672CB00010B/1962